How to Build
A Magnetic
Church

Creative Leadership Series

How to Build A Magnetic Church

Herb Miller

Creative Leadership Series
Lyle E. Schaller, Editor

Abingdon Press / Nashville

How to Build a Magnetic Church

Copyright © 1987 by Abingdon Press

This book is printed on acid-free paper.

Library of Congress Cataloging-in-Publication Data

Miller, Herb.
How to build a magnetic church.
1. Church growth. I. Title. II. Series.
     BV652.25.M55   1987   254'.5   86-28782

ISBN 0-687-17762-6 *(soft alk. paper)*

8/03

"Little Gidding" by T. S. Eliot from *Collected Poems 1909-1962*. Used by
permission of Harcourt Brace Jovanovich and Faber & Faber Ltd.

Scripture quotations in this publication, unless otherwise noted, are from the
Revised Standard Version of the Bible, copyrighted 1946, 1952, © 1971, 1973
by the Division of Christian Education of the National Council of the
Churches of Christ in the U.S.A., and are used by permission.

Scripture quotations marked KJV in this publication are from the King James,
or Authorized, Version of the Bible.

MANUFACTURED BY THE PARTHENON PRESS AT
NASHVILLE, TENNESSEE, UNITED STATES OF AMERICA

c.l

Dedicated to the NET Resource Center team, the kind of people who climb the impossible mountains to change the world:

Margo Woodworth

Marvel Maunder

Nicki Johnston

Richard Roland

Grace Ferguson

Karen Medlin

Marlene Hutton

Suzanne Hyman

Patti Rohde

Kelly Smith

Foreword

Between January 1, 1880, and the end of 1906 the Disciples of Christ organized nearly four thousand new congregations. The Methodist Episcopal Church and the Methodist Episcopal Church, South launched a combined total of sixteen thousand new churches in that twenty-seven-year period. The National Baptist Convention (Colored) founded more than twelve thousand new congregations in that same era. The twenty-four Lutheran denominations in existence in 1906 reported that nearly eight thousand Lutheran parishes traced their origins to that period. A combined total of sixty-five hundred new churches were organized during those twenty-seven years by a dozen Presbyterian denominations. The Protestant Episcopal Church reported in 1906 that approximately three thousand of their 6,845 parishes had been organized in those years. Sixteen Baptist denominations reported they had organized a combined total of twenty-eight thousand new churches in those years. Fifty-eight hundred new Roman Catholic parishes were organized in that period.

The four denominations who eventually came together to form the United Church of Christ started a combined total of nearly four thousand new congregations in those years.

The Church of the United Brethren in Christ, a relatively small denomination with only 275,000 members in 1906, organized nearly eighteen hundred new churches in that era—an average of approximately seventy new missions each year! By contrast, the ten million member United Methodist Church organized an average of twenty-five new congregations annually during the 1970s.

Well over one-half of the 213,000 religious congregations in existence when the census of religious bodies was conducted by the United States Bureau of the Census in 1906 reported that they came into existence during those twenty-seven years.

That era represents the peak years of new church development by the "oldline" denominations of American Protestantism. Those were the days when the operational policy for reaching more people with the good news that Jesus Christ is Lord and Savior was to start more churches. This was the central strategy for reaching the millions of new immigrants from Europe, for serving the blacks freed by the Civil War (more than twenty-five thousand new black congregations were organized in the four decades following the close of the Civil War), and for evangelizing the Western frontier. It was generally assumed that the most effective means of reaching more people was to organize more churches. The strategy worked. Three dozen different denominations doubled, tripled, or quadrupled their membership in the forty years following the end of the Civil War.

During the 1960s that strategy was largely abandoned by most of the long established Protestant denominations, with the notable exception of the Southern Baptist Convention. Today the central component of a church growth strategy in most of the older Protestant denominations is not to organize a large number of new congregations, but rather to encourage existing congregations to reach more people. Experience has demonstrated that that is a difficult undertaking. One reason is that it calls for a radical shift in priorities for the allocation of scarce resources. Another is that it requires an internally generated desire to change. A third is that it requires the exercise of a new set of habits and skills.

That is what this book is about. It is a lucid, creative, and powerful account of how to build a magnetic congregation that attracts people. The vast majority of long established congregations are, unintentionally in most cases, designed to repel newcomers. This is a natural, normal, and predictable tendency of most long established organizations. In nine brief chapters, each filled with creative suggestions on what to do and how to do it, Herb Miller suggests an approach that can transform the inward looking congregation into a vital and magnetic church that attracts *and keeps* newcomers.

Like other volumes in the Creative Leadership Series, this book has been written for use by both pastors and lay leaders who are seeking help as they carry out their responsibilities as faithful servants of God.

In an era when encouraging existing congregations to grow has replaced new church development as the primary means of reaching more people with the good news, this volume stands out as a practical, provocative, readable, and useful evangelistic tool.

LYLE E. SCHALLER
Yokefellow Institute
Richmond, Indiana

Contents

Introduction

Johnny's bright eyes were fixed on the plastic Scotty dogs he held in each small hand. As he brought them close to each other, they jumped together with amazing power. Again and again he pulled them apart and watched with fascination as they instantly united. Turning them over, he studied the metal platforms on which each dog was mounted, looking for the magic. The mystery remained hidden. Some invisible, yet powerful, force inside these tiny dogs pulled them together with tireless repetition.

With regard to membership totals, three kinds of churches inhabit the North American continent. One kind is magnetic, regularly attracting more new members each year than it loses by death, transfer, or shift to inactive status. Another kind is neutral, attracting about as many new members as it loses. A third kind repels, losing a few more members each year than it gains. How does the magnetic congregational personality differ from other churches? Like the Scotty dogs, the internal power hides from casual observation. We must excavate the life-styles of many such churches before the hidden forces become apparent. The nine chapters in this book list the nine most essential of these magnetic factors. Churches lacking one or more of these can still provide effective ministry. But during our particular era of American church history, they will not be magnetic, growing congregations.

G. K. Chesterton and several literary friends gathered one evening to enjoy some stimulating intellectual conversation. One of them posed a hypothetical question: "If you were isolated on a desert island and could have only one book, what volume would you choose?"

One guest replied, "The complete works of Shakespeare." Another said, "I'd choose the Bible."

When Chesterton's turn came, he said, "I would choose *Thomas' Guide to Practical Shipbuilding.*"

For most church leaders, a description of the nine invisible magnetizers that influence the flow of new members is interesting, but insufficient. "How can we perform *magnet transplants* in neutral or repelling congregations?" they will ask. Each chapter, therefore, suggests methods for moving beyond conceptual analysis into practical shipbuilding.

I

Throw Your Message to Wider Receivers

Recognize that a denominational label on the lawn is no longer enough to produce membership growth.

A new trend walks the hallways of American Christianity. Born in the turbulent 1960s, this baby grew to teenhood in the "Me Generation" of the seventies. It became a giant in the "Baby Boomers Returning to Church" wave of the eighties. By the late 1990s, congregations whose leaders fail to make course corrections will view this trend as the "Incredible Hulk" that crushed their futures while they were sleeping. By 2010, some of the mainline denominations, victimized by this trend before they knew what hit them, will have shrunk to numerical shadows of their former sizes. Looking in 2030 rearview mirrors, church historians will wisely note that those denominations died the natural death of all institutions that refuse to face reality.

The most recent United States Census Bureau reports estimate that 16.6 percent of Americans change their place of residence each year. Many of these persons move within the same county and continue to attend the same church. Of those who move farther away, *approximately one-half join churches of a denomination different from the one they previously attended.* In the Christian Church (Disciples of Christ), for example, 56.5 percent of all new members who joined by transfer during 1984 came from other denominations.[1] Other mainline communions report similar figures, especially among their growing congregations. A study in The United Methodist Church indicates that new members in their fast-growing churches are far more likely to come from non-United Methodist backgrounds than is the case in their nongrowing churches.[2] The woman pastor of a fast-growing black congregation in Denver says, "Of the seventy persons added to our rolls in the last three years, only four transferred from a congregation in our own denomination. Only three others had ever attended one of our denomination's churches." Check this statistic in your own congregation. Ask fellowship dinner attenders to raise their hand if they formerly belonged to another denomination. Or tally up the denominational origins of the persons who joined your church last year. Your immigration figure will fall somewhere between 40 and 75 percent, depending on your denomination and your geographical location.

This "transfer ecumenism" is a radically new behavior. In 1965, eight out of ten Methodist church members said they had always been Methodists. Eighty-five percent of all Baptist church members had always been Baptists. Three-fourths of all Lutherans had always been Lutherans.[3] American pastors have strongly preached Christian love, tolerance, and ecumenism since World War II. Now, mainline churches find themselves in the same position as did first-century Jews. For a thousand years, their prophets had said the Messiah was coming. Yet, he arrived in such an unexpected form that most of them missed him. While pastors and denominational leaders were writing study documents and attending meetings on how to unite their churches, laypersons went ahead and did it—but in an unexpected way. They stopped paying attention to the labels on the lawn. While many of them disdained organic church union, they started practicing inorganic church union. Ecumenism by mixture is now outdistancing ecumenism by merger.

This new behavior by American churchgoers has several ramifications. First, it gives some congregations an "edge" over others. Churches that aggressively seek new members tend to grow. Passive congregations that assume moving members will seek them out tend to shrink. Forty-two percent of Americans attend worship each Sunday—compared to 37 percent in 1940—but a large slice of this group has come unglued from denominational loyalty.[4] They decide where to go to church on the basis of criteria other than denominational labels. Churches that meet those invisible criteria are growing. Those that do not are dying.

Second, this new ecumenism forces church leaders to scrutinize their congregational life from a new perspective. During the 1970s, American automakers awakened to a new world. Rising oil prices and inflation rates fueled new buying behavior. Prior to that time, our auto manufacturers had been competing only with themselves. Suddenly, imported automobiles forced radical introspection and significant design changes. American congregations are facing a similar crisis of shift in public behavior. But because churches are not under stockholder pressure to measure their effectiveness by the financial "bottom line," leaders have been slower to recognize the crisis proportions in their new environment.

In his early career, Gautama Buddha served a wealthy prince. One day, a palace aide brought Buddha an inquiry from the prince. The prince wanted to know the single most

17

important advice Buddha could give about administration. Buddha said to the servant, "Tell him to begin by defining the nature of the problem." In American denominations, the nature of the problem has altered. People join churches for reasons other than the sign on the lawn. Many churches whose behavior in the 1980s is like their behavior thirty years ago will not be alive thirty years from now.

The Old Ways Fail in New Days

Earlier in this century, mainline denominations relied on three highly successful numerical growth methods: denominational evangelism, biological evangelism, and architectural evangelism. At that time, people moved from state to state less frequently. When people moved, they found a sense of home and safe security in joining churches with familiar labels. Their natural human tendencies toward competitive aggression would later in this century find expression through television football. In that earlier era, they often found outlets in pen and paper diatribes hurled against competing denominations. Even judicatories that preached Christian unity tended to practice Christian exclusiveness. By unity, they meant, "Everyone should join us." During that high birth rate era, large families of children often grew to adulthood in the same town. (When that continues for several generations, you can grow large congregations in a few decades.) All over America, that happened. No wonder people felt secure in "architectural evangelism." They could sit in their pews and say to one another, "Everyone in town knows where the church is." Much of the church growth came effortlessly—by procreation, population expansion, presence, cultural acceptance, and perpetuation of institutional life.

The depression years of the 1930s began unraveling this familiar fabric. People moved elsewhere for jobs. World War II completed the change. People moved throughout the

United States. By 1960, the birth control pill appeared, and the new convictions about enjoying a "quality life," which replaced older ideas about the quantity of family, encouraged its use. The live birth rate shrank to 15.9 per one thousand population in 1982 from its post-war high of 25.3 per one thousand population in 1957 and 30.1 per one thousand population in 1910. This "double whammy" of all families getting smaller and many families moving away suddenly placed many stable mainline churches in a pattern of decline. Those in small towns found their members moving to the cities. Those in downtown locations saw many of their members departing for the suburbs. Paradoxically, the trend toward smaller families was linked to a surge in population. The post-war "baby boom" peaked in 1961, with 4.2 million live births (compared to 2.8 million live births in 1911 and 2.3 million live births in 1933). The biggest generation of young adults in history appeared at exactly the time Americans were beginning to feel flexible about their denominational affiliations.

Added to this new sociology was a new theology. Sick of fighting and family separations, the soldiers who made it home from the beaches of Normandy hit American shores with a new mood of religious tolerance. Instead of, "We can unite if you join us," they were declaring, "Let's cooperate." This mood gave birth to the National Council of Churches and to the World Council of Churches. Conversations about Christian unity began between numerous fractured church bodies. Enmities born in pre-Civil War days began healing. Presbyterians, Lutherans, and others started moving toward one another rather than apart. By the 1960s, even the head of the Roman Catholic Church was encouraging a new sense of ecumenism. By October 1981, only three of every ten lay respondents in a Lutheran Church in America *Listening Post* poll felt there was anything unique about Lutherans that distinguished them from other Christians.[5] By April 13, 1986, this new spirit of tolerance had arrived at such a stage that Pope John Paul II could make the first recorded visit by a pope to a Jewish Synagogue. What was unthinkable in the 1920s became "do-able" in the 1980s.

Many other factors fueled this "transfer ecumenism" trend. One was an escalating divorce rate. Divorces per one thousand jumped from .9 in 1910 to 5.3 in 1981. Experts predict that by 1990 more spouses will be part of a second marriage than of a first. People do not choose their new spouses on the basis of denominational affiliation. This marital mixing bowl accelerates the denomination-hopping trend.

Earlier in this century, many young people attended denominationally-related private colleges rather than state universities. The community colleges to which they commuted from their homes had not yet appeared. By 1965, the likelihood of meeting and marrying someone from the same denominational background had reversed itself into the likelihood that marriage would occur between persons of *different* religious affiliations. Persons born in the 1956–60 era are twice as likely to be involved in an interfaith marriage as persons born in the 1920s.

By 1965, new divisions of competitive viewpoint had replaced the boundary lines formerly drawn between denominations. Now, conservatives in the Presbyterian Church are far more likely to have something in common with conservatives in The United Methodist Church than they are with liberals in their own denomination. New alliances have formed. Ideology has become more important than denominational signs and symbols. Instead of seeing themselves as members of denominations, Christians see themselves as members of congregations and subscribers to particular ideologies within American Christianity.

By the 1980s, another homogenizing influence had

appeared: the ecclesiastical "McDonaldizing" of America. Congregations of different denominations increasingly obtain their programmatic materials from identical sources— outside denominational structures. Some examples are: adult Bible study materials from The Bethel Series in Madison, Wisconsin, and Trinity Bible Studies in El Paso, Arkansas; lay training in pastoral care from The Stephen Series in St. Louis, Missouri; stewardship materials from Pony Express in Oklahoma City, Oklahoma; youth ministry materials from Christian Youth Club in Monroeville, Pennsylvania, and Group Magazine in Loveland, Colorado; continuing ministerial education from the Albin Institute in Washington, D.C., and the Yokefellow Institute in Richmond, Indiana; research insights regarding congregational vitality from Lyle Schaller in Chicago.

The old days are gone, and we are not just at the wrong end of the pendulum. These new days are an arrow flying from a bow to which it will not return.

Ecclesiastical Mid-life Crisis

When people stopped thinking in terms of labels on the lawn, they became willing to join denominations they had not previously considered. Between 1973 and 1983, the Southern Baptist Convention grew 15 percent. The Church of Jesus Christ of Latter Day Saints grew 40 percent, the Assemblies of God grew 71 percent, the Seventh-Day Adventists grew 34 percent, and the Church of the Nazarene grew 22 percent. Membership in fundamentalist churches jumped more than 35 percent. Orthodox Jewish congregation membership rose 100 percent. During the last ten years, membership rolls in mainline Protestant churches fell 8 percent. Weekly Mass attendance among Roman Catholics dropped by one-third. Mainline church bodies constituted 73 percent of America's Protestant population in 1920 and only 49 percent in 1985.[6]

By the mid-1980s, many denominational executives were feeling like the two women golfers who were greeted by an ebullient "pasture athlete" who had just finished nine holes of golf with a better-than-average score. "Good afternoon," he said. "Hope you had a good score."

"I would rather tell you my age and weight," one of the women replied grimly.

Since the early 1960s, The United Methodist Church has lost about one-fourth of its membership. The Presbyterian Church (USA) has lost 27 percent of its membership since it began declining in 1966. The Christian Church (Disciples of Christ) has lost 33 percent of its membership since 1964. These declines have slowed, but have continued through the past ten years. The Presbyterian Church (USA) registered a net loss of 354 members every day between 1971 and 1975. During the 1979 through 1983 years, that daily net loss slowed to 138 members. But that means they were still losing the equivalent of one Presbyterian Church every two days.[7] Other slower, but continuing, declines include losses of 3 percent in the Lutheran Church in America between 1973 and 1983, 4 percent in the Episcopal Church, and 13 percent in the United Church of Christ.

A psychologist was preparing to see his first patient of the day. Sorting through the stack of charts on his desk, he realized that his first patient, someone he had never seen before, was eighty-six years of age. As the psychologist began to get acquainted with her, he said, "Tell me, what brings you to see a psychologist at this particular stage in life? I don't see many persons of your age."

"Mid-life crisis," she replied.

Due to sociological, psychological, and theological shifts in American thinking, mainline churches started slipping into a mid-life crisis during the 1960 decade. But this mid-life crisis, like those experienced by individuals, is not all bad. As Benjamin Franklin said, "Those things that hurt, instruct."

Decisions made during this critical period can have positive results. Old habit patterns can be discarded. Previously unthinkable alternatives can be examined. New roads can be taken.

Roadblocking Myths

Several myths tend to block the reconstruction of mainline denominational road patterns by its leaders. For example, a prevalent view states that theologically conservative churches can grow, but theologically liberal churches cannot. While the record indicates that this tendency is accurate, other parts of the record show that this is an inaccurate generality. Many growing mainline churches are liberal in theological orientation. Church growth comes not from conservatism but from *extroverted* conservatism. Not all conservative churches are growing. Only those having an extroverted orientation toward the estimated 49.7 percent[8] of American citizens who are unchurched are growing.

A second myth declares that people join churches that tell them what to believe. The record indicates that young adults are more interested in churches that have sharply defined beliefs and identity. Yet, they also join theologically open and diverse congregations in large numbers, providing those congregations are extroverted rather than introverted.

A third myth indicates that television is drawing people away from churches. Gallup Poll studies have corrected that inaccurate perception. People who watch religious television are, for the most part, deeply involved in their churches and remain so.[9] People who watch football on television are the same people who attend football games in stadiums. People who don't like football neither watch it on television nor buy season tickets.

A fourth myth says that Sunbelt churches are growing and

that since many Sunbelt churches are Southern Baptist and more conservative, they naturally have the edge on numerical growth. While this perception contains some truth, the generality is not accurate. Studies of fast-growing churches in various denominations indicate that many are in the Sunbelt, but many are also in Rustbelt northern states where population growth is zero. A growing population area does not automatically spawn growing churches. Churches grow more easily when the population is booming, but that does not guarantee growing churches. Swimming downstream with a fast current of population growth is easier. Swimming upstream against a declining population is tougher. But if you do not know how to swim, it does not matter which direction you swim.

Saturated with these unfortunate myths, many mainline church leaders have been blocked from recognizing the opportunities in their mid-life crisis. They are like the pilot who came out to talk to the upset passengers, who had been sitting on the runway for three hours in the airport. Thunderstorms had half the air traffic locked on the ground and the other half making big circles in the sky, waiting to land. The pilot said to the disgruntled passengers, "I have some bad news for you. We are fortieth in the line of planes waiting to take off. But that is not the worst news. The tower is not letting anyone take off."

This gloomy situation has caused an unfortunate unecumenical overreaction against conservative churches by many leaders in the nine declining mainline denominations. Their murmurings sound a little like the invocation a retired chaplain gave several years ago at a ballgame between two denominationally-sponsored teams. After praying all the things one usually hears in such athletic prayers, he surprised everyone with these words: "Lord, if you can't help us tonight, please don't help the Baptists."

24

We Can Choose Our Future

Inventor Charles Kettering once said, "Of course I'm interested in the future. I expect to spend the rest of my life there." Mainline church leaders who do not become intensely interested in the future will thereby make it exceedingly short. A statistician in one of these denominations says that if its numerical decline of the last twenty-two years is projected into the future, A.D. 2027 will be the signpost at the end of the road. During that year, two members will remain of the former two million. One will die from cardiac arrest due to overwork. The other will give up and join a Southern Baptist church.

But the future of a church is far more determined by the priorities and direction of its leaders than by its past performance or present circumstances. The past twenty-five years is forever finished, but the future can still be shaped. The old, sheltered days are gone. Church leaders can no longer count on the automatic allegiance of the masses to denominations and traditions. They must deal with shifted needs and perceptions. But mainline churches can still have a positive future—if they face these new days with new plans.

II
Is Your Church Inviting?

*Learn how to attract large numbers of first-time worship
visitors.*

A couple entered a cafeteria in which they had eaten at least
twice a week for several years. Glancing across the parking lot
at a small shopping center next door, the husband remarked,
"Look, someone has put in a barber shop over there."

The next day, he came back to get a haircut. "I saw your sign
yesterday," he said to the barber. "How long have you been
here?"

"About five years," the barber replied.

"How can that be?" the man said. "I have been eating fifty
yards from here for years and never knew you were here."

"We just put up a barber pole a few weeks ago," the barber
explained. "The name of my shop is *Scissor Wizard*, so a lot of
people thought we sharpened scissors here."

People seldom join churches until they attend at least once.
The average church loses 6 to 7 percent of its members each
year by death, moving away, and drift to inactivity. That

pushes the attracting of new people to the worship service beyond a "good idea" status to a "necessity" status. Why, then, do church leaders not work harder at it? The three big causes of membership anemia already noted in chapter one contribute to this neglect: overreliance on denominational evangelism, on biological evangelism, and on architectural evangelism. But at least ten other factors play major roles.

The first of these ten factors is a lack of theological motivation. A pastor said, "We have a lot of turnover from the military base, but our membership holds about even each year. Why would we want to do an evangelism program?" Paul answers that question this way: "So we are ambassadors for Christ, God making his appeal through us" (II Cor. 5:20). People in our community have deep needs that Jesus Christ can meet. God empowers us with the Spirit when we act as his ambassadors. Leaders of every church base their outreach efforts on one or the other of those opposite theological perspectives. One leads to active extroversion, the other to passive introversion.

The second reason members do not work at attracting new members is the failure to see that the factors that influence people to attend a church the first time are quite different from the factors that influence them to attend a second time and to eventually join. Working hard at one of these two tasks cannot compensate for doing nothing with the other.

The third factor is the *inactive member fallacy*. When the subject of new member recruitment comes up, at least one respected leader will say, "Before we go out and try to get a bunch of *new* people, I think we ought to try to get back the people who already belong but no longer attend." On the long list of inaccurate clichés church people exchange with one another, this one ranks near the top in destructive potential. No church grows by concentrating on its inactive member list.

Thanks to the pioneering research of John S. Savage, we now know why church members become inactive.[1] Thanks to the "Reunion Training" provided by the organization Savage heads—and thanks to a program titled "Coming Home for Christmas," developed by a Christian Church (Disciples of Christ) organization—we now know how to get the small percentage of inactives to return who are ever going to return.[2] More important, we now know how to prevent members from becoming inactive. But we can attract ten new members to our church with about the same amount of energy it takes to get one inactive person to come back. New member recruitment and inactive member work are two different subjects. Both are important, but neither can substitute for the other. Both should be worked at, but in very different ways.

The fourth is an unconscious shift in focus from *making* disciples to *serving* disciples. Many churches operate like a factory whose goal is to manufacture personal Christian growth, while forgetting that this process cannot begin without new persons. Making people more Christian and making more people Christian are as distinctively different as are obstetrics and pediatrics. Both are necessary aspects of health care, but neither can substitute for the other. Pastors of growing churches give leadership to both without assuming that either is a by-product of or a substitute for the other.

The fifth is the *spiritual versus numerical growth fallacy.* "We want spiritual growth, not just numerical growth," a lay leader said. "We concentrate on quality, not quantity." That proud declaration sounds prophetic, but it is closer to pathetic. In church life, quality and quantity are far more likely to be blood relatives than enemy tribes. Churches that are not growing numerically are often not growing spiritually either. Bob Burt, evangelism executive for the United Church of Christ, says, "An increase in size tends to produce an increase in quality in several areas—the congregational singing, the quality of choirs, the quality of church schools, the quality of lay leadership, the quality of youth ministries, the quality of

28

community outreach, the quality of study groups, sometimes even the quality of preaching. Growing churches usually find that an increase in size produces an increase in the quality of ministry."[3]

Sixth is the erroneous assumption that "everybody in our town already has a church home." Church membership, as a percentage of state population, ranges from a high of 60 percent in the New England states to a low of 34 percent in the Pacific states.[4] But nowhere between the two ocean boundaries do we hear of a town in which *everyone* attends church.

Seventh is the predominantly rural perspective of many church leaders. Seventy-six percent of the American population now lives in metropolitan settings. Yet, because many church leaders grew up in rural settings, they make outreach decisions through those mental lenses. Raymond J. Bakke, of the Lausanne Committee for World Evangelization, says that the same problem plagues Christian expansion efforts throughout the world.[5] The rural mentality of churches causes their members to expect people to come to them, without their needing to use any methods of attraction.

Eighth is the *let your light so shine fallacy*. This distorted interpretation of Matthew 5:14-16 says that if you live an exemplary Christian life, people will see your good works and want to become Christians, themselves. Close scrutiny reveals that this is the religious version of an old secular saying: "If you build a better mousetrap the world will beat a path to your door." That was never completely true of mousetraps, and it is not true of Christianity. A Christian's life-style rarely by itself produces new Christians. Christianity is communicable, but is seldom caught visually.

Oscar Wilde once said that his Aunt Jane died of mortification when no one attended her grand ball. But she died without knowing she had failed to mail the invitations. This happens in many fine churches. They have wonderful worship services and splendid programs, but fail to tell people

29

outside the walls that this party is for them. James said that faith without works is dead (James 2:17). Faith without words dies, too, or it never gets born.

The ninth factor is just plain selfishness. Why is constructing a church building so much easier than building a congregation to put in a church building? Because growing a church takes unselfish extroversion. Church members can erect buildings from the motive of selfish introversion, but evangelistic outreach requires going outside ourselves for the benefit of other people.

The final factor is the *let's not play the numbers game cliché*. On the surface, that slogan sounds like high virtue. Down deep, it is shallow. Warren Hartman, head of research for The United Methodist Church, says, "The numbers game has often been replaced with the 'leave them alone' game"[6] This new game is equally as dangerous and unbiblical as is the game it replaced. By leaving people alone, we are: (1) deciding not to care about them, which violates the Great Commandment, and (2) deciding not to care what Jesus told us to do, which violates the Great Commission.

How can a church define itself as a church without trying to attract new members? That contortion would require the rejection of numerous New Testament passages—Luke 15:1-32, John 3:17, Luke 5:1-11, Matt. 9:36-38, Matt. 28:19-20, and John 20:21. Yes, numerical growth can become ideological idolatry if a church makes it the *only* goal. But leaving evangelism off the priority list is an opposite and equal heresy. The New Testament repeatedly reports numerical growth in the early church (Acts 2:41, 47; 4:4; 5:14; 6:1, 7; 9:31; 11:14, 20-21; 16:5). However, growth was not the primary objective. Christ was. But growth was a result of that focus, and they celebrated what they saw God doing.

The Planning and Services Research Department of the Southern Baptist Convention has studied the fastest-growing churches in that demonination. One of ten observations made by researchers David and Phillip Jones is that "numerical growth is receiving priority in the fastest-growing churches to a greater extent than the typical churches . . . the fastest-growing churches do think about numbers."[7]

Ultimately, the question of whether we should seek to attract first-time worship visitors comes down to one of authority. On what authority do we intend to base our church's priorities for ministry? If we build only on personal opinion, we can decide to exclude efforts to attract new people. Or we can decide to define these efforts in such distorted ways that we don't have to work at them. Charles Allen, the United Methodist pastor and author, said, "Not one time does Jesus command people to attend church. Do you remember one instance? I don't. But he had a lot to say about people going out into the highways and hedges and finding people."[8] Jesus said, "Go ye . . . " (Matt. 28:19). That sounds like an imperative rather than an option.

The Best Method of Attraction

Lutheran Church historian Martin Marty says that one word defines the difference between churches that grow and those that don't: **invite**. Marty reports a study that indicates that the average Episcopalian invites someone to church once every twenty-eight years.[9] His statistic may be an exaggeration, but his point is not. When a church isn't growing, its members are not "inviting."

A study of the new members who joined the Christian Church (Disciples of Christ) during 1984 tells us that 77.6 percent of them attended the first time because of "relational influences"; they heard about the church through a friend, an acquaintance, or a relative. These 77.6 percent break down into fifteen different categories. Only 5.6 percent attended for the first time through the influence of a minister or of family.[10] This study confirms the everywhere-quoted maxim

31

from the Institute for American Church Growth in Pasadena, California: 70 to 90 percent of persons who join any church in America come through the influence of a friend, of a relative, or of an acquaintance. No amount of theological expression from the pulpit can overcome a lack of invitational expression from the pews.

A pastor called on a young couple for six years. They were always pleasant and said they planned to attend, but they never did. In the sixth year, a layperson who knew the husband invited him to play on the church softball team. He was an excellent pitcher, and the team started winning games. A few weeks later, the family attended church. Three months later, they joined. Three years later, he was elected to chair the board. There you have it: A dedicated, faithful, capable, theologically trained, evangelistically oriented pastor visited for six years—nothing. An untrained, friendly layperson who likes softball visits for one week—success!

A small bank in Cumbria, England, had only two employees, the manager and a teller. Even on a busy day, customer traffic was not enormous. One day, no one came in at all. Finally, at 3:30 P.M., the manager told the teller to lock the front door. Minutes later he returned and said sheepishy, "It *is* locked. We forgot to open it this morning."

Invitations are the way churches open their doors. In the ministry of attracting first-time worshipers, forget about drawing a square on a map around the church and trying to "serve the people in our neighborhood." There are virtually no "neighborhood churches" left in America. When people started driving cars, they began picking churches relationally, not geographically. Only 12.3 percent of new members are influenced to join by a church's location.[11] If your church is within fifteen minutes driving distance of people's homes—the travel comfort zone for American church attenders—they are in your parish. How do you pick your personal friends? By drawing squares on a map? People choose their churches the same way they choose their friends because of the relationship they have with someone who invites them to attend. That is why the newest members make the best inviters. They know more people who do not at present attend any church.

How to Invite

In almost any conversation, it is easy to ask, "Do you regularly attend a local church?" Do not ask whether a person belongs to a church; that tells you nothing. If that person does attend a church, your question leads to an interesting conversation. If he or she does not, say: "I would like to invite you to attend our worship service." Make a date to take that person to church or to meet in the narthex and sit with him or her.

In extending such invitations, do not confuse harvesting with planting. People go through five stages on their way to church membership: awareness, conprehension, interest, desire, and action. When we invite people to church, we are working with the awareness (planting) stage. A basic agricultural principle is that you cannot harvest something until it has been planted. Ninety-five percent of all effective evangelistic interactions involve planting, not harvesting. The harvesting never happens on the same day and is seldom done by the same person.

What about inviting people who have become inactive in another congregation? Many of them will at some point start attending another congregation, and few will return to the same one they left. When inviting inactives, be prepared to do much listening, especially if they feel close enough to talk with you openly. Many became inactive because of a painful event that broke their relational bond with the pastor, the key leaders, or the other members. Let them talk. Encourage them to express feelings with responsive listening statements, such as, "You feel like. . . . " When they finish their stories,

33

you may want to ask if they feel that they can forgive the person or persons involved and make a fresh start. If they say, "Yes, I can forgive, but I don't think I can ever go back to church there," take them seriously. Most of them mean it and will act it out. If that is their response, you may want to ask something like, "Do you think the deep pain you have suffered will cause you to break your relationship with Christ and weaken your Christian commitment?" Then invite them to attend your church. Tell them your own feelings about the importance of church attendance.

In every kind of invitational conversation, avoid preaching, lecturing, judging, ordering, shaming, or indiscreet probing. Do express concern. Be willing to listen and take the persons' needs seriously. Be vulnerable. Let them know you are not perfect—unless you are perfect, in which case you will not have to tell them; they will have already noticed. Be willing to share your faith meekly, not as a perfect answer, but as an answer that has worked for you. More people become part of God's kingdom because of love than by rational persuasion. We don't argue people into the church; we love them into it. Reverend Monsignor William McCormack summed it up in a Roman Catholic study: "The appropriate approach in evangelization should be 'to propose, not impose.'"[12]

Motivating More Members to Invite

Qualitative factors in the church climate greatly influence the quantity of invitations members extend per week. As Lyle Schaller has observed, people tend to invite when their own faith is growing, when they like their pastor, and when they are excited about what is happening in their congregation.[13] But few growing churches rely on spontaneous enthusiasm alone. Most of them also use some kind of systematic encouragement to motivate members to invite. In some ways, these specific plans are synthetic. They cannot substitute for spontaneous inviting, but they do raise consciousness. They help members to see people they could invite, and members involved in these systematic plans usually increase their number of spontaneous invitations. Practice builds ability, which builds confidence, which builds results.

Whatever plan of systematic inviting is undertaken, avoid two sand traps: (1) *The let's study evangelism trap.* People who study evangelism without simultaneously taking action on what they are studying do not always move on to action. The studying often becomes a substitute for the action. When they finish studying the evangelism course, they often want to study something else. In studying evangelism, concurrent action is the key to learning. (2) *The evangelism committee trap.* Involve a large number of persons from the congregation, not just the evangelism committee. In most churches, this committee is locked into a no win task. Its members cannot possibly succeed by themselves. The evangelism committee is not like the property committee or other functional committees, which can often complete their ministry tasks by using labor from within the committees themselves. Evangelism committees, no matter how hard they work, cannot achieve their goals by working alone. They must build a bigger net.

Prayer Invitations

A fast-growing United Methodist church in Richland, Washington, has used the following method twice a year for several years. A few weeks before Christmas and Easter, the pastor schedules five minutes of meditative background music in the morning worship service. After the ushers distribute 3" X 5" cards, the pastor asks worshipers to write down the names of everyone they can think of who does not attend church. He then asks them to pray for those people every day for the next two weeks. During morning worship two weeks later, he urges worshipers to invite to church those people for whom they have been praying. Average worship attendance has grown from three hundred to twelve hundred during the past dozen years.

In using that idea, a pastor can help people get in touch with their many opportunities for invitations by reading the following material at the beginning of the meditative moments:

"It is good for us to stop and consider what persons God may be calling us to reach out to on his behalf. I am asking each of you to use the next few minutes to make a list of the persons you know who are not actively involved in a church, especially those you feel you may be able to influence. To help our memories, I will review several categories of persons with whom each of us has contact:

- Think of family members—spouse, parents, grandparents, aunts, uncles, cousins, in-laws, nephews, and nieces.
- Think of neighbors—next door neighbors, elderly persons in the neighborhood, and new families on the block.
- Think of persons you know through sports or hobbies— people with whom you bowl, golf, or play tennis.
- Think of people at work—supervisors, employees you supervise, secretaries, clerical staff, students you teach, clients, new staff members, and colleagues you see once in a while.
- Think of friends with whom you dine out—single friends, parents of your child's friends, old friends from school, and friends of your spouse.
- Think of casual associates—your dentist; your doctor; your realtor; your life insurance agent; your child's teacher; merchants; service or luncheon club members; persons who belong to clubs, associations, or professional groups you attend; babysitters; sales representatives who call on you frequently; and persons who graduated from the same university as you.

• Think especially of persons who are undergoing personal life stresses of some kind. These individuals often find helpful answers to their problems from within the Christian faith—persons who are recently divorced, families with new babies, families that have experienced a recent death, families in which someone has lost a job or has suffered painful business reverses.

Personal Delivery Letters

Fast-growing Signal Hill Evangelical Lutheran Church, in Belleville, Illinois, perfected a method of attraction they call the "Personal Delivery Letter." Pastor Henry A. Simon describes it this way:

> Regular church goers sometimes speak with disdain about "C and E Christians"—members who come to church only on Christmas and Easter. Yet, the appeal of Christmas and Easter festival worship for infrequent attenders can also be used for an evangelism outreach. . . .
>
> That is the premise behind the "Personal Delivery Letters" which members of our congregation hand deliver to persons targeted for outreach before Holy Week each year. . . .
>
> The method is simple. On the second Sunday before Easter Day, our members are asked to hand deliver an invitation to persons on our outreach list. The addressed envelope, stamped "Personal Delivery Letter," includes a letter of invitation from me (personalized by a P. S. if at all possible) and a schedule of our services from Palm Sunday through Easter Monday. The letters are passed among worshipers in our offering plates, to show that personally delivering the invitation is an offering of time, energy, and effort to the Lord. Worshipers take a letter and deliver it before the next Sunday. Extra envelopes without a name and address are available for members (guests have used them, too) to deliver to someone not on our outreach list. . . .
>
> We stress that all a person needs do is say, "Hello, I'm John

37

Smith from Signal Hill Evangelical Lutheran Church. This is a personal delivery letter for you." Some persons who would blanche at the suggestion of making an evangelism call will take a personal delivery letter. . . . A member may not take a personal delivery letter, but may be moved to ask a friend, relative, or acquaintance to attend our special worship services during Holy Week and Easter. . . .

Letters for persons in *outlying neighborhoods* will be taken by our evangelism callers and congregational officers beforehand. That will enable us to tell worshipers that all *their deliveries* are [close by].

We will once more ask people not to sort through the letters, looking for a nearby address. We have normally done this, but forgot it in 1984. One person stopped an offering plate for more than a minute as she searched through the letters.

We will remind persons that letters cannot be placed in the addressee's mailbox. This is against postal regulations. Letters can be put between doors or left in some other visible place—but not in the mailbox.

The same Lutheran congregation developed an "Outreach Christmas Card" version of the same idea. Several churches of other denominations successfully imitated it last year. They designed a specially printed card containing the times of the Christmas Sunday and the Christmas Eve Candlelight Carol services. Members take the cards to mail to their unchurched acquaintances. The church name, address, phone number, and weekly service times are stamped on the back of the envelope in which the cards are enclosed.

Open House Invitations

A Disciples congregation in Perryton, Texas, developed a much copied "Open House Sunday." Usable any time of the year, it is particularly appealing when used to kick off fall programming in September. Tracy Wilson, the senior pastor, describes the process like this:

At least two weeks before Open House Sunday, the pastor preaches a sermon on evangelism, stressing the importance and effectiveness of persons influencing their existing friends, relatives, and associates who do not have an active church home. . . . On at least one Sunday (two is better) and no later than two weeks before Open House Sunday, distribute commitment cards during morning worship and set aside time during the service for their completion as an act of worship. Commitments are made to try to influence specific acquaintances toward Christ and our church—to pray for them, to strengthen friendships with them, to share one's faith with them, and to invite them to church (particularly to Open House Sunday). These cards are signed and *kept* by the persons completing them as a reminder.

On the Sunday before Open House Sunday, the pastor preaches a sermon on Christian hospitality, lifting up God's will for the treatment of strangers ("foreigners") in our midst. . . . So many of our people do not know how to reach out to strangers, nor do they realize the Christian imperative. . . to do so or the difference such effort can make. . . .

The entire church membership is encouraged to invite friends and associates for Open House Sunday. Because a free, *catered* dinner will be served at lunch time immediately following worship for all guests and members, reservations are to be turned in at the church office. . . .Each member who is bringing a quest(s) will turn in his/her name(s) so food arrangements can be made, and so the church can be aware of guests' names prior to their arrival. . . .

On the morning of Open House Sunday, the pastor preaches a sermon on the theological beliefs and uniqueness of our church—"What We Believe."

As part of worship, a brief but thorough outline is presented of all the programs and activities of the local church. . . . This information is good for everyone to hear!

Following worship, a free catered lunch is served. There is no program at the luncheon, only a time of fellowship and the announcement of how glad we are that guests have come. . . .

39

As everyone leaves, they are given printed matter describing the [denomination and local church]. . . .

On Monday, a letter is sent to guests. . . . A visit from a church member within the first forty-eight hours following Open House Sunday can be beneficial.

"Bring a Friend Sunday," used by hundreds of congregations during the last five years, is similar to Open House Sunday. A pastor in Mulvane, Kansas, says, "In five years, we have had a total of 275 visitors to worship at our five Bring-a-Friend Sundays. Many of these persons subsequently joined our church and became active members."

Second-best Methods of Attraction

Since 22.4 percent of new members will visit worship the first time because of something other than a personal invitation,[14] we should also use the nonpersonal methods listed below. But impersonal methods of attraction are dangerous to church health if used as substitutes for the more effective personal methods. Churches that rely on media methods alone for attracting first-time worshipers decline in size. Advertising cannot replace personalizing. Use nonpersonal attraction ideas only as supplements to personal invitations, not as substitutes.

The Building and Sign. Since 6.9 percent of first-time worship visitors show up becuase they saw the building, take another look at yours.[15] The pastor of a growing church in Pacific Grove, California, says, "We have been putting our historic Victorian building into top shape so passers-by know we care about our church. The outward appearance of the building speaks of the inward condition of our church soul."

Place church signs perpendicular to the street and raised off the ground, if possible. Light them at night. Small town churches benefit from signs on the major highways entering the community. Churches built off the main thoroughfares in larger communities need signs directing people to their existence and location. Size and upkeep are critically important. Signs too small to see or shabbily kept are worse than none.

A denominational executive wanted to attend church in a new community. The beautiful building was valued at three million dollars, but the signboard gave no time for the service. He scanned the newspaper and telephone directory but found no answer. He did not worship there that Sunday because he could not find out when to arrive.

The Yellow Pages. Increasing morning worship by an average of only one person per year ordinarily adds between five hundred and one thousand dollars to church income. Move up out of the one-line ad to a two- or three-line small box. The Yellow Pages are an expensive place to save money.

Radio. Sixty-second spots aired five days per week during the time when people drive to and from work are a good use of media money. They are especially cost-effective in smaller towns, where radio rates are cheaper and local stations reach all age groups. Airing Sunday worship services, except for very large churches in metropolitan areas, is *narrow*casting rather than *broad*casting. Few unchurched persons flip on their radios to catch a church service. Sixty-second spots, on the other hand, reach out to everyone.

Don't preach. Focus on life-situation and inspirational themes. People are bored and repelled by doctrine. They are attracted if the "radio window" into church personality offers acceptance, warmth, and need-meeting answers to life stresses. Some pastors have the skill, discipline, and large blocks of time to write their own spots. Most ministers find it more practical to subscribe to a syndicated script service, like *Radio Bright Spots.*[16] An Indiana pastor says, "*Bright Spots* bring us an average of five new worship visitors per Sunday and tremendous recognition in the community. Two people I did not know stopped me in a local market last week and told me

41

how much they appreciated a recent spot. The church board is urging me to find new stations to expand it."

Television. Thirty-second spots are the best length for TV. But these are seldom a live option unless the church is huge, affluent, and metropolitan. Spot packages are available from several denominational sources. Some commercial companies make demonstration tapes and printed scripts for TV spots, which a pastor and local station can produce inexpensively.[17]

Newspaper. Saturday or Sunday newspaper listings of worship service times have value, but not as much as Yellow Page ads or radio spots. Larger, boxed ads have limited power in large cities, but can be practical and financially feasible in small communities in which everyone reads the local or county paper. For the best impact, sequence the ads weekly during September, the Christmas season, or the Easter season, rather than monthly throughout the year. Some denominational offices produce excellent ads. Others produce ads that communicate with national staff members but not with the public. Some commercial companies also produce inexpensive ads.[18]

Direct Mail. A few congregations use direct mail to residents of particular zip code zones. Most experts say that each mailing must contain a minimum of five thousand pieces in order to be effective. The Orthodox Presbyterian Church in Mechanicsville, Pennsylvania, sends a quarterly mailing to thirteen thousand homes. The pastor stresses the cumulative effect of the mailings. A church in Gowen, Michigan, sends a thirty-five-hundred-piece mailing four to six times each year to nearby homes. The material slants toward the interests of the readers and the desire to serve them, not toward the need of the church to obtain more members. A third of the visitors come as a result of these mailings.

Large, one-time mailings do not have the impact of smaller, repetitive mailings. A California congregation sent out forty thousand cards advertising its worship services and offering free child care for two hours each week. Only eighteen persons responded. Only two visited the worship services, and no one asked for child care.

New Residents. A few churches, mostly in smaller towns, have developed effective means of contacting new residents. A church in Aiken, South Carolina, developed an inexpensive card and plastic envelope/door hanger to leave when people are not home. On one side, the card has an invitation to church. On the other, it has a map of how to find the church, along with times of services and a picture of the pastor.

Several commercial companies provide newcomer address lists.[19] While relating to new residents is effective in some small communities, avoid the newcomer fallacy. An overdependence on this method results in low or no growth. During the 1950s, mainline churches started concentrating on "all those new people moving in." This shift is one of several reasons for their numerical downfall.

If new resident mail contacts are used without home visits, at least three mailings are necessary. A pastor in Stow, Ohio, describes the process like this: "A real estate agent provides us with a list of deed transfers in our area. Some of our members who are limited in mobility feel very useful in addressing envelopes for this important ministry. We include a cover letter, a brochure, and a response card. After this initial mail contact, we mail twice more during the next two months. Each mailing contains the weekly newsletter that carries our monthly calendar. Apart from members bringing their friends and neighbors, this is our most fruitful outreach for first-time visitors, many of whom have placed their membership here."

Moving Member Hotlines. One denomination now has a toll free number by which addresses of moving members can be transmitted to churches across the state or continent. Others are setting them up. These should be helpful, since research indicates that a high percentage of new residents do not continue their denominational connection in the states to which they move.[20]

What Business Are We In?

Church leaders, by their priorities and actions, continually illustrate what business they have decided they are in. Some are in the sheep business. Others settle for being in the sheep shed business.

Jesus said in the Great Commission that we should go into all the *world* (Matt. 28:19). Notice that he did not say we are to go into all the *church*. Leaders must continuously ask themselves, "What business are we in? Are we in the church business or the world business? Are we in the institution business or the people business? Are we concentrating on a mission-evangelism-extroversion focused ministry? Or have we settled for a nurture-maintenance-introversion focused ministry?"

Jesus says to the leaders of every church, "Go into all the world and make disciples." Without recognizing the theological incongruity of their response, members in churches of every size, from micro to mega, tend to say to one another, "Our church is about the right size." Why? Because people usually feel more comfortable with where they are now than with where God is calling them to be. Picture Paul and Barnabas sitting in the coffee shop at the Holiday Inn in Antioch. They are meeting this morning to plan the missionary expansion of the church. Paul says to Barnabas, "You know what I think, Barnabas?"

"No," Barnabus says, lifting his coffee cup. "What?"

"Our church is about the right size."

That does not fit Paul, does it? He was always looking across the fences of his personal comfort zones—toward Corinth, toward Rome, toward the whole world beyond. He never settled into a safe harbor, because he never forgot what business he was in.

III
God's Power Plant

Provide a positive, uplifting worship service.

Sally told her friend Margaret about a great movie and urged her to see it. Margaret went Friday night. At first, she was bored. Then, she was irritated at having wasted her money and time. Halfway through, she walked out.

A wide majority of new church members visit worship the first time because a friend or relative has invited them. *But this is not the reason they return a second time and eventually join.* They come once because of a friend's judgment. They return for a second look because of their own judgment. Only 9.7 percent of new church members indicate that having friends who belong to the church was an important reason for joining. The friendliness members extend to worship visitors is one of four major reasons they give for returning a second time and for eventually joining. But the quality of the worship service is the primary determiner: 82.7 percent of new members rate it as an important reason for joining.[1] If the worship service fails to meet the needs of first-time attenders, no amount of friendliness can convert them to joiners.

A little boy spent a summer weekend at a nature camp. When his mother picked him up, she asked the usual motherly, "How was it?"

"Okay," he said. "But they played tricks on us."

"What do you mean?"

"Like when they made us get up every morning for ravioli, then didn't give us any!"

When people get dressed up for worship, we must give them some. If we don't, they look elsewhere, especially in the nation of comparison shoppers, which American churchgoers have become. Andrew said to his brother, "Come and see" (John 1:39). When Peter came, he saw Christ. After we invite people, they must see Christ in the worship service. Otherwise, the invitation proves phony. They come and do not see. Then, they go elsewhere—or nowhere. The sequence goes like this: (1)We invite people to come and see Christ. (2) After they have come, we invite them to meet Christ. (3) After they have met Christ, we invite them into the Christian family with friendliness. (4) After we have invited them into the family, we accept them into the family by making a place for them in the group. (5) After we have accepted them into the family, we ask them to become involved in inviting others to come and see Christ. This process can get blocked at any of the five points. But the worship service is the most invisible block. The home folks become so easily convinced that "the way we have always done it is the way we should always do it."

During the last two decades, many pastors have studied and developed counseling skills. More people than ever now appear in pastors' offices to seek help with personal problems. Yet, recent research says that during times of crisis 80 percent of adults attempt to work the problem out on their own. Eight in ten of them turn to prayer, and 64 percent seek support from the Bible or other inspirational literature. Formal sources of support, such as a professional or religious counselor, are sought by only a small minority of the masses.[2]

Harry Emerson Fosdick said decades ago that worship services are like group counseling. Worship is still one of the primary ways people find help in dealing with the rigors of life. No wonder its quality has so much influence on church choice. No wonder 64 percent of dropouts in one mainline denomination cite "worship service is not meaningful" as a major cause.[3]

A Family Feeling

Mainline denominations are victims of poor timing in their liturgical development. During the mid-section of this century, those with unsophisticated rural origins began trying to mature beyond their backgrounds.They succeeded. Compensating for the individualistic excesses of the revival era, mainline denominations became more rational and less emotional. This struggle brought many improvements to worship services. But mainline denominations reached their zenith of formalism two decades late. They achieved dignity at exactly the time that a new generation of baby boom young adults was searching for a sense of family and "feeling" in worship services.

What kind of worship service meets people's needs today? The pastors of 177 significantly growing congregations across North America were asked what qualities they strive for in their worship service. These quotations typify their responses:

"We strive for *warmth* as well as *dignity*."

"We strive for a kind of relaxed dignity."

"We try to have a warm, friendly type of worship without it's being too folksy or losing dignity."

"We strive for a warm formality."

"Orderly flow with flexibility."

"Joy with dignity, expressed affection, a happy, upbeat climate."

"Warmth and flexibility."

"A blend of informality and centeredness."

"We strive for a spirit of warmth and family during worship."

"We try to create a friendly family life atmosphere that demonstrates our caring fellowship."

Describing the service in her declining church, a laywoman said, "Our congregation's formal formality has become cold formality. If people wanted that, they would do their worshiping in a doctor's waiting room." People look for worship services that communicate a warm, family feeling. Is this because people who experienced that in their growing up years want to reexperience it in their church family? Is this because people who did not experience it in their formative years have been searching for it all their lives? Whatever the reason, when they meet it in a church sanctuary, they come back for more.

Joys and Concerns

The sharing of joys and concerns in morning worship is a common thread in growing mainline churches. Their pastors say this is one of the principle ways they achieve a family feeling.

"Many people are attracted by the informal sharing of joys and concerns prior to the prelude."

"Providing a time for sharing joys and needs before the morning prayer is important to us. We are careful not to hurry that time, but let all share. And they do."

"I begin with a brief 'greetings and announcements' on the lower level before we begin our worship *per se*. We sometimes sing 'Happy Birthday' to someone. Such intimacy, I believe, allows the Spirit to be more effective in its work in our worship experience."

Children Mean Family

More and more young adults appreciate institutions that emphasize family qualities and values. The baseball industry tied into this by declaring 1986 the "Year of the Family." Another trend is the increasing respect for each individual person and a desire to meet his and her needs. This contrasts with earlier generations, who focused on meeting the needs of the majority of persons in a particular group. These two trends have increased the number of congregations that use a children's sermon or children's church, or both. These churches are not just following a fad; they are responding to a deeply felt need. At a time when families are disintegrating at the fastest rate in recorded history, the statement, "We care about families," sounds like good news.

Humor

Research among cancer patients points to the health-giving value of humor. If that is true, according to the following statements, by pastors, growing churches are health havens:

"I think humor is a big factor in saying we accept people."

"When you don't have to worry about how you look or what you say, that means you belong. Humor is one of those symbols."

"We have a fast-paced worship service focusing on humor, hope, and enthusiasm."

Pastors in growing churches act as elevator operators; they help raise spirits to God's floor of optimism and joy. So, when in doubt, smile. Don't look grim. Don't take yourself too seriously. Several of your parishioners had parents who did that for years. They do not need it from you.

Indigenous to the Culture

The dictionary defines *indigenous* as "having originated in and being produced, growing, living, or occurring naturally in a particular region or environment."[4] However you define it, indigenous worship is essential to effective evangelism. People appreciate a slightly different type of worship service in Roaring Branch, Pennsylvania, from that in University Church, Tampa, Florida. Worship leaders unaware or uncaring about needs indigenous to their particular culture reap the reward of empty pews.

This need for indigenous worship is especially obvious in black congregations. When black pastors imitate white worship styles in attempting to fit into mainstream culture, they lose traction in their own unique culture. A black pastor in Boston says that the worship style of whites is desired by some blacks, but is not effective for the masses of black Americans. "Here in the Northeastern Jurisdiction, many black churches have taken on traits of the majority churches," he says. "But we can't worship like whites and attract the masses. Some white leaders are against hand-clapping. They call it charismatic."[5]

A pastor attended an ecumenical worship service in Kingston, Jamaica. A Jesuit priest had composed music for the complete Roman Catholic Mass in Jamaican rhythmic style. The use of indigenous music is a helpful tool everywhere the church flourishes on the world's mission fields. The same principle applies to the various subcultures across North America. Rather than trying to impose ideas gleaned from seminary days or from music appreciation courses, leaders of growing churches go with the flow of what works here and now. Their ancestors did the same thing on the American frontier when mainline denominations were growing rapidly. They fit the worship clothing to the people, not the people to the pastor's preferences and prejudices.

What type of people are you trying to reach in your worship service? People over fifty-five? People who have been members for thirty years? Young adults? People outside the church's walls? Both? After these questions are honestly answered, you can easily answer the next ones: "How do we meet the worship needs of this particular group? How can we help these people move into the presence of God?

Variety Is the Spice of Live Churches

Boredom is the root of much evil in church life. Nowhere is this more true than in worship. Something new grabs attention and recharges commitment. Sameness, sameness, sameness sends the mind to the sandman! The law of "diminishing responsiveness to sameness" causes retail merchants continually to redesign their shelf displays. "If you want to change the response, change the stimulus," they say.

Growing churches conquer boredom by creatively varying the parts of a general worship service format that remains the same:

"We have a structured worship with variations within that structure."

"We use a variety of individual worship expressions."

"We make changes in worship from time to time to keep it from becoming stale."

"We make some innovative alterations in the order of worship each quarter."

"Our service is very traditional, but we regularly have innovations in the service, when they are deemed consistent with the goal of that particular service."

Growing churches develop structured variety. Dying churches develop routine ruts. The older the average age of members, the harder leaders must struggle to achieve variety.

Since 65 percent of persons in many mainline denominations are over the age of fifty, the natural pressure of majority opinion runs many worship services downhill toward resistance to change. This soon becomes a self-fulfilling preference. In a few years, the church has only older people in its services.

Scheduling two morning worship services is one of the best ways to add variety. Adding a second service usually increases total attendance by 5 to 15 percent. A simple principle stands behind that universal statistic: Offer more options, and you get larger responses. People who are intimidated by large crowds can join the church during the early service. Those who like informal worship can attend another service. People who like something shorter can attend that one.

Churches often fail to take advantage of the visual in their efforts to create variety. A new science called *neurolinguistic programming* claims that people receive communication in three ways: visually (through seeing), audibly (through hearing), and kinesthetically (through feeling). Different people have different dominant learning (communication receiver) modes. Some learn best by hearing. They often say, "Listen to this," or "I hear you." Others learn best by seeing. They often say, "Look at this," or "I see what you mean." Others learn best by feeling. They often say, "You can sense that this is true," or "I know how you feel." Since worship serves all three kinds of people, use variety in all three communication modes. Otherwise, you end up bringing only one or two kinds of persons into the presence of God. Make worship services visual experiences (with colors, movement, pageantry). Make them auditory experiences (with sermons that communicate truth in compelling, interesting ways). Make them kinesthetic experiences (with hugs, handshaking, music, a children's sermon, fellowship moments). And give each part intentional variety.

Accelerate the Tempo of the Music

Since music is 40 percent of the service, the tempo can either resurrect or murder all other parts. Americans prefer bright, happy, cheerful music. When the music is upbeat, visitors get a feeling of liveliness and creativity, rather than solemn sameness. Live music arouses enthusiasm (the word *enthusiasm* means "filled with God"). By contrast, dead music fills people with sleepiness.

Worship leaders often overlook the laws of physics. When people sing with a piano, they wait for the pianist to strike the chord before they sing the words. The delay caused by the sound of the chord traveling to the ear, to the brain, and finally to the vocal chords is detrimental to creating a festive mood in worship. This problem is further compounded if the accompanist waits for the congregation instead of trying to play ahead. It can become an even greater disaster when the accompanist is playing a pipe organ, due to the delay from the time the key is pressed until the sound emerges from the pipes. All this only takes a split second, but in our world of technicolor, technisound, and technieverything, split seconds can seem like years. Americans are accustomed to watching a week go by in thirty minutes and a year in one hour. A hymn that drags can seem like an eternity and destroy any hope that the noise we make to the Lord sounds joyful.[6]

Possible solutions: (1) train someone with a good singing voice to sing *before* he or she hears the chord rather than after. Station this individual at an appropriate position in front of the congregation and have him or her lead out in the singing. (2) Make your choir members aware of the problem. Ask them to practice singing each Sunday's hymns on the beat rather than after. (3) Ask the organist to select three people of three different ages from the congregation (not from the choir) to meet with him or her for five minutes following worship once a month. This group keeps asking and answering the question,

"How is the tempo going?" Feedback is the "breakfast of champions." But if you never ask, you never get fed.

Sing Hymns We Know

Choir directors in growing churches do not try to make worship services into music appreciation courses. Hymn singing is not for the benefit of musicians, but for the edification of believers. The most important question about church music is, "Does it move people closer or further from God?" To overcome the problem of accidentally singing hymns the congregation does not know, appoint a task force of eight persons, evenly distributed across the age range of twenty through eighty. Ask this group to meet and go through the hymnbook, making a list of "all the hymns we presently know." Take this "approved hymn list" to whoever selects the hymns for each Sunday. (Threaten him or her with loss of life and limb if the list is not used.) This procedure allows leaders to teach new hymns intentionally, instead of accidentally.

Multi-generational Appeal

The greatest need for a truly multi-generational experience is not in Christian education, but in worship music. Almost every congregation contains three musical generations each Sunday morning. One group (many of whom are over the age of forty) prefers "classic" hymns, like "The Church's One Foundation." A second group likes music from the gospel era, much of which was written between 1900 and 1935. Many of these persons are over sixty years of age. This music was popular when they were young—the period when people develop their likes and dislikes for music. A third group enjoys contemporary Christian hymns, many of which have been written or set to a different tune since 1960. They also like contemporary choral responses. Many of these persons are under forty years of age. Growing churches try to meet the musical needs of all three groups of people in every service, not just occasionally. They know that focusing on one kind of hymn results in several people leaving the service feeling as if they have not been to church. Worship and music leaders who choose to serve only one kind of worshiper will, after ten or twenty years, end up with only that kind of person in their services.

Some churches need to trash their old hymn books—either because they are ancient and contain only gospel hymns, or are newer and contain only the classic hymns. A young attender at a national denominational event wrote on the evaluation form, "Sing a variety of hymn styles next year. I felt stoned to death by the rock of ages." Many church members would like to scream the same objection, but nobody gives them a chance. Today's twenty-five to forty age group has grown up with faster, rhythmic tunes and the sharp tones of guitars, saxophones, and drums. Communication with this generation means learning to speak their language. The hymn cadences and sonorous organ tones of the 1950s often make younger ears sleepy.

Experiment for a few months with a hymn selection formula that involves one classic hymn to open the service, one hymn selected from the gospel era, and one from the contemporary church music scene. Sprinkle in some additional responses of a modern variety. Evaluate with a questionnaire circulated among morning worship attenders. If you buy a new hymnbook, get one that contains all three types of hymn—the classic, the gospel, and the contemporary.

How long must churches keep revising their music in order to meet changing needs? Forever! Tastes in music keep changing.

Live Preaching

The pastor read his brilliantly worded sermon in a slow monotone. His hands clenched the pulpit as if it were threatening to slide away. He glanced up at the end of each paragraph as if to assure himself that his parishioners were still there. Had he looked more carefully, he would have seen that they were not.

The seminary training of many mainline pastors prepared them to write manuscripts rather than to communicate with people. Research in public speaking at Brigham Young University helps us understand what happens when pastors read their sermons. Fifty-five percent of a speaker's impact comes from *visual* qualities (the way he or she looks, acts, and gestures). Thirty-eight percent of a speaker's impact comes from *auditory* qualities (vocal tone, articulation, speed, cadence, volume). Only 7 percent of a speaker's impact comes from the actual content of what is said.

Many components contribute to the total mix of a worship service experience: friendliness and enthusiasm of the congregation, quality of the music, form and flow of the service, the building's architecture, the decor of the sanctuary, the bulletin's appearance, evidence of active programming, availability of parking, and the church's reputation in the community. However, nothing influences the worship service as much as the personality and style of the pastor.[7] That is not communicated primarily by the content of what is said but by how it is said. The effective communicator comes across "live," not on "paper cassette recordings."

Beating the Ecclesiastical Energy Crunch

New Testament Christians engaged in five activities: worship, learning, fellowship, witnessing, and service. Each of the last four derives its motivational energy from worship. Mainline churches tried to manage with substitutes for this vital force. Their membership declines show how well that worked. "Evangelism is more atmosphere than program," Carlton Buck said decades ago. His granddaughter, also a pastor, commented at a recent worship workshop: "Do we hatch eggs in a refrigerator? No, an incubator." If the worship service is not warm, indigenous, varied, upbeat, joyful, positive, relational, need-meeting, multi-generational, and live, how can the Christian faith hatch in a new generation?

56

IV
Forward to Basics

Emphasize biblically based preaching and teaching.

In 1977, 23 percent of Roman Catholics in the United States said they had read the Bible within the previous thirty days. By 1986, that figure had risen to 32 percent.[1] One out of every four adults in the total population of the United States currently participates in some form of Bible study group. Younger adults (ages eighteen to twenty-nine) are involved at approximately the same percentage levels as older persons.[2] What is happening here? The gigantic young adult segment of the American population is reclaiming the biblical authority base that their grandparents never left, but that many of their parents did. The growth rates of several denominations have benefited from this renewed appreciation for the biblical message as the centerpiece of Christian faith. After experiencing a vacuum of Bible-focus in their childhood denominations, many young adults responded to the biblical preaching and teaching they heard in the Assemblies of God, Church of the Nazarene, Charismatic, and Community Bible churches. T.S. Eliot put it this way:

We shall not cease from exploration
And the end of all our exploring
Will be to arrive where we started
And know the place for the first time.[3]

Many mainline pastors protest with, "But not all preaching that sounds biblical is biblical! And some preaching that is biblical does not sound biblical!" While obviously true, that defense misses the point. The young adults are saying, "The preaching had better *sound* biblical, or we will not hang around and try to figure out whether it *is* biblical." They expect sermons to contain a high percentage of Bible-based content. The preacher can throw in poetry, humor, psychological insights, and quotations from great literature, but young adults expect the central point and framework to arise from a biblical foundation. They do not respond to sermons that use a biblical text as an introductory diving board from which to jump into a pool of philosophical observations.

Mainline pastors find this new preaching preference hard to accept for two reasons: (1) Their own personal experiences as young adults were the exact opposite, and (2) they saw young adults earlier in the century doing exactly the opposite. "Don't we all know that maturing young people move from being right-wing theological conservatives to left-wing theological liberals?" they ask. But that trip is no longer typical of young adults. Many of them now move away from the left-wing liberalism they grew up with toward a right-side evangelicalism. If they do not get biblically based preaching in buildings whose labels are familiar from childhood days, they look elsewhere.

Many pastors have recognized this trend. After a twenty-year sojourn of making bricks in the Egypt of rational positivism, psychologism, self-helpism, and social actionism, they are now leading their people in reclaiming this biblical promised land. Church historian Martin Marty, in commenting on the congregations in The United Methodist Church that are showing vitality and numerical growth, notes a consistent "back to the basics" theme. He sees a "re-tradition-ing" going on, not the kind that promotes a romanticized gimme that ole time religion," but a return to worship, preaching, and study within the basic Wesleyan biblical traditions.[4]

A questionnaire asked pastors of growing congregations, "What is the theological focus of your preaching and teaching?" Their responses verify Marty's observations:

"I find that basing a message on biblical texts and illustrations gives added strength. This does not mean dogmatism but an appeal to understanding God's will."

"I spend a lot of time studying the Bible and time with people, and I seek to bring the resources of our faith to bear on human needs. I am intentional about submitting us to the judgment and the inspiration of the Scriptures."

"I love and am committed to the biblical message, both the Old Testament and the New. I believe this message, studied with careful scholarship and proclaimed in such a way as to speak to modern needs and problems, can still today have transforming power."

"Yes, But" Preaching

Bible centered preaching is gradually replacing a homileti-cal style whose proponents viewed it as scholarly, while not recognizing that their hearers saw it as sterile. A layperson describes that antique mainline style: "Some time ago I visited a congregation across town. The minister had the right degrees. He wore the correct color stole. The sanctuary would seat six hundred, but fifty-eight were present. I, age sixty-five, was one of the younger persons there. He preached on "The Documentary Hypothesis of the Pentateuch," along with

59

"Why Mark Didn't Write Mark"—all in fifteen minutes. No wonder our churches are going down the tube, and should if they follow this procedure."

A mainline seminary dean, whose denomination has shrunk by more than one million members in twenty years, wrote a magazine article about the Christian faith. While he undoubtedly intended to instruct rather than to degrade, he seemed to look down his nose at students who attend university religious groups that "specialize in believing the impossible and having a warm heart." He moved on to three illustrations of how dangerous it can be to take biblical passages literally. This kind of "yes, but" approach to biblical truth grew out of "form criticism" scholarship popularized earlier in this century by German theologians. While fascinating to intellectual types, it tires normal minds. Few young adults will stand in line to learn what is wrong with the Bible and what it does *not* say. Faith comes from hearing the Word (Rom. 10:17), not from hearing scholarly criticisms of the Word. A "yes, but" articulation of Christian faith does not reproduce itself in the real world. Fortunately, the "form criticism mania" generation of scholars is coming to an end.

All preachers, if they are honest, have some doubts. But why advertise them in the pulpit? A surgeon uses many kinds of instruments. But when entering a waiting room to talk with the family, the surgeon does not carry tools along for a medical "show and tell." The family wants to hear whether the patient will live or die, not how complex appendectomies are. Preachers use many excellent academic tools to learn biblical truths about life. Those who display their toolboxes in the pulpit—instead of the truths—should be sued for malpractice.

Antidote for Burnout

Research by the Alban Institute shows that 23 percent of Protestant church leaders are suffering from burnout and

that another 19 percent are living on its borders.[5] One of the
several causes of this problem is the tendency to load
megabytes of responsibility on leaders, but to give them little
opportunity for the spiritual strength that comes from Bible
study and prayer development. "Man shall not live by bread
alone" Jesus said (Matt. 4:4). Church leaders cannot live by
committee meetings alone. Committees provide fellowship
and strengthen personal values. No church can achieve its
ministry goals without them. But taken by themselves, they
are like a diet of all carbohydrates and no protein.

A renewed conviction about the need for Bible study is also
the key to brightening mainline church school attendance
fadeout. The more than 70 percent attendance losses in many
Sunday schools cannot be reversed by better teaching
methods. Nor does the solution lie solely in the need to pump
in more enthusiasm, friendliness, extroversion, or new
curriculum. *The revitalizing of Sunday schools cannot occur until
leaders recover their convictions regarding biblical authority.*
Without a strong belief that the Bible has something
authoritative to say to every human creature on earth, why
would we feel compelled to teach it to children, or to anyone?
The argument between educators who want to call it church
school and those who want to call it Sunday school is a waste.
We ought to call it what it deserves to be called—Bible school.
We could then call our traditional once-a-year experience
summer Bible school.

Interpreters Should Interpret

A pastor sitting in an all-night restaurant at 5:00 A.M. was
studying her sermon notes in preparation for the early
service. Through the low background noise of the restaurant,
she became aware of a lyric melody coming from the cook's
radio in the kitchen, close to his counter. The music was soft
and beautiful, but the words were in an unfamiliar language

she had never heard before. She wondered what message the notes carried on their lilting wings. At that moment, a waitress came by and refilled her coffee cup. As if reading her mind, the waitress said, "That is a beautiful song. I just wish I understood the words."

Pastors engage in at least nine ministerial roles. But more than anything else, they are interpreters. If they do not deliver on this, their major task, who will?

V
Set Your Thermostat on Friendly

Exhibit an attitude of "welcome home" friendliness toward nonmembers.

The pastor was astonished at his welcome. He had just arrived at an ancient Coptic monastery out in the desert, nearly a day's journey from Cairo, Egypt. The monks treated him as if he were the one important guest they had been awaiting since the place was established in the twelfth century. They served a fine meal, showed him to a comfortable room, and brought him a bouquet of flowers. He was then greeted by the abbot of the monastery, Father Jeremiah.

"Wow!" said the pastor. "You sure know how to treat visitors."

Father Jeremiah replied, "We always treat guests as if they were angels, just to be safe."

Some of that scene is repeated each Sunday in the more than 340,000 American churches. Among the people who gather for their familiar worship routines, a few new faces appear. These visitors are not all angels, and it is difficult to identify instantly just what they are. Some are strangers in the

night, passing through town. Another is somebody's grand-
mother, visiting from Toledo. A few are deeply troubled
people, looking desperately for God's help. But some are a
special kind of angel. Two years from now, one or two of these
visitors will be the most active leaders in the church. They will
become committee chairpersons, tithers, and congregational
drive shafts—providing, of course, that church members
make them feel comfortable the first Sunday they attend. If
not, they will seek spiritual haven elsewhere.

Warren J. Hartman, research director for The United
Methodist Church, says, "When both unchurched and
churched people are asked what they look for in a
church . . . all of them agree about one factor—the climate of
the congregation. They are looking for a church in which they
feel at home, where the people are friendly, and where there
is a warm and comfortable atmosphere."[1] Congregations
cannot grow without an atmosphere of love. Warmth attracts.
Ice cools both lemonade and people. A cold church, like
butter, will not spread. Growing churches have learned how
to regulate the congregational thermostat and they have set it
on friendly.[2]

Churches have always needed friendliness, but cultural
changes have made that quality more essential today than
earlier in the century. The congregate society of small town
America, in which everybody knows your grandfather and
your uncle, has vanished. Most Americans now live out their
lives in a consumer society. The principle objective in most
human interactions is to use people in some way, rather than
to relate to them. This produces feelings of loneliness, which
make love and acceptance much more important to American
churchgoers now than in the 1950s, when many attended
church for the benefit of their children.[3] Psychologists say that
a lack of connectedness is the most universal symptom they
currently see in counseling offices. In the 1950s, it was
anxiety. In the 1960s, it was loss of identity. In the 1970s, it was

depression. In the 1980s, it is lack of connectedness. Friendliness is the antidote for loneliness and disconnectedness. When you find it, you latch onto it.

Pastors of growing churches say that friendliness plays a key role in their congregations:

"Our people make visitors welcome. Couples greet the visitors when they come in, and most of the members go to them after the service. Almost all of our visitors tell me they have never experienced such love and warmth in other churches."

"As pastor, I make a concerted effort to speak to every visitor at the door and at the coffee fellowship and have repeatedly asked our people to do so. I speak often to the congregation about speaking to the visitors first, and to their friends later."

"When people leave our congregation after visiting for the first time, they often say how friendly the group is and how different it is from other churches they have visited."

"I believe people are hungry for caring, unselfish love and that God works through people to provide that love."

Ecology is a branch of science concerned with the interrelationship of organisms and their environments and the interaction among different kinds of organisms. In the ecology of church life, coldness is like acid rain. God's grace is always sufficient, but when our grace is not sufficient, we block people from experiencing his. The following factors help congregations develop a positive ecclesiastical ecology.

Warmth in the Pulpit. A woman in a declining church wrote on a consultant's data-gathering sheet: "A family that is shopping for a church home has visited our church a couple of times. I was behind them in line after the service when they reached the pastor. He turned away and was talking with someone over in the coat room—with his hand limply extended to these visitors. He never did acknowledge their presence. Would you choose this as your new church home?" Unfortunately, this was not an isolated incident in her congregation, but a repetitive behavior pattern. Church people tend to take on the attitudes, style, and behavior modeled by their leader. Ice in the oven retards the baking process.

An Effective Greeter Corps. Words printed on a button worn by a waitress at the Holiday Inn in Youngstown, Ohio, are: "You're My First Concern." Are worship visitors your church's first concern? The way leaders act out the answer to that question determines whether worship visitor numbers increase or decrease. Recruit a greeter corps. Station two greeters at each door, warm individuals who work at remembering names and faces. Ask them to arrive fifteen minutes early. They should serve prior to Sunday school as well as before and after worship. Avoid asking one of the existing church groups to take on the greeter responsibility, nor should you use members on a rotational basis by going down the alphabet of last names. Both of these commonly used systems have a built-in 75 percent failure ratio. With either process, about half of your greeters will prefer not to do this work. They will then act out their passive aggression by low enthusiasm, showing up late, or not showing up at all. The other one-fourth will be sincere, but untalented at greeting people.

Select and recruit persons you feel would be highly competent in this work. Pick gregarious, outgoing people who have good social skills. Have them meet together for an initial training session at which they go around the room sharing one or two of the worst experiences they have had in visiting congregations. While they tell these stories, have a recorder make a list of behaviors you want to avoid in your congregation. The pastor and other leaders can then add

66

specific points that are important because of your particular building, experiences, or location.

Extroversion in the Pews. Some churches open their doors to the public. Others open their hearts. Visitors instantly sense which is happening. Ask church board members to assume responsibility for the pew or pews in the area of the sanctuary in which they sit for worship each Sunday. They are usually willing to welcome and get acquainted with any strangers who appear in these pews, providing they commit themselves to such a covenant. This will ensure that no one can leave your worship service and say, "Not a single person spoke to me." After this plan is launched, remind the board members of it several times each year. Bad habits, like weeds, hang on tenaciously. Good habits do not flourish without occasional fertilizing and watering.

A California pastor illustrates the solution to another common problem: "We organized 'secret hosts.' As the crowd moves from the sanctuary into the coffee hour after worship, these three or four,couples watch for people who are standing alone, talking to nobody. This got started because a man who visited our church said to me, 'Young man, you're not gonna make that church grow. It's the coldest I ever saw. I went to the coffee hour and stood around. I spoke to people, and nobody seemed to care where I came from.' Within a month, we had secret hosts."

At a large church in Arizona, greeters take first-time visitors to a registration center. There, they are given a large packet (8" X 10"), which contains information about the church and a book written by the pastor. The church leaders watch for people who are carrying these packets, which are too big to stick in pockets. That way, numerous members make it a point to welcome them, without needing to worry about accidentally welcoming a long-time member returning for a visit. Anyone who has a packet is a visitor.

Mixing Bowl Moments in Worship. Some churches install a

three-minute fellowship spot in the worship service, when the pastor, choir members, and other worshipers wander about greeting people. Some churches do this at the beginning of the service. Some churches do it before the pastoral prayer. Some do it before the closing hymn. While a few older members may say it breaks up the sense of worship, most persons find it adds warmth by breaking down the natural timidity and sense of isolation that many people feel in large crowds.

Stay Loose Before the Service. Forget the myth that you need total silence before the service begins; some things are worse than sound clutter. The quietest churches are those in the middle of big fights. Let people visit. Organize some silence into the early moments of the service. You can control that, and everyone can participate.

Large Narthex. Winston Churchill once said, "We shape our buildings, and then our buildings shape us." The amount of floor space immediately outside the sanctuary greatly influences friendliness and fellowship. If people have a comfortable place in which to hang around and visit, they will. If not, they tend to go straight home. Some large, older churches need to remove the last few pews in order to provide this space. Some long-term traditionalist members will scream. Let them. Better to hear them complain in a full building than an empty one.

Coffee Fellowships. An after-worship coffee time is another way to improve warmth and friendliness. When members and greeter corps workers urge visitors to stay for coffee after worship, many will. If they get acquainted with a few people, they feel more like returning next week.

Name Tags. In many larger congregations, plastic name tags for everyone help both new and older members learn names more quickly and thus increase the friendliness quotient. Name tags say to newcomers, "We expect new people in our midst and want you to feel welcome." Getting older church members to want to wear name tags requires persistent effort and education regarding the "why" of the idea. Some of the same people who fully understand why they wear name tags at Lion's Club lunches have trouble understanding why we need them at church.

Socializing Sessions. The pastor of a fast-growing church in Virginia says, "When the evangelism chairman's list of real prospects grows to about a dozen, we throw a party at one of our member's home. Prospects are cordially invited and sometimes picked up and brought to the party. We treat them royally. After refreshments, we sit down and talk about our faith and what our church means to us, but mostly we listen and appreciate the ideas and interest of prospective members."

Information Sessions. The larger the church, the more beneficial is some kind of information session. A growing church in Texas uses a two-session "Beliefs and Practices" class. A growing church in Washington state uses a four-session class (repeated monthly) that meets on Sunday morning and occasionally has an alternate all-day Saturday format. A Dallas congregation hosts a Visitor's Information Meeting each month, which adult classes take turns hosting. They send written RSVP invitations with stamped, return reply cards. Over 70 percent of attenders join the church within the next two weeks.

Nursery Quality. Is your church nursery equipped for young parents? North America is currently experiencing an all-time high in the number of young women who are mothers for the first time. Their expectations regarding satisfactory child care facilities are higher than those of their mothers twenty-five years ago. These young women grew up with carpeted floors, air conditioning, and modern bathrooms. A poor nursery climate, due to personnel problems, old furniture, shabby paint, or lack of cleanliness, is a way of saying, "We are not expecting company and are not concerned about making you feel comfortable here."

69

Adult Sunday School. Many adult classes come across as cold to visitors. An effective greeter is just as important here as at the front door of the building. Recruit one individual in each class to serve as the official greeter. Choose someone who meets strangers easily and is never at a loss for words. This greeter should arrive early. Sunday school visitors who walk into a cold, empty room in which the lights are not yet turned on feel less than impressed.

Young Adults. In a Nebraska congregation, young people babysit in the church nursery during lunch some Sundays. This gives young couples an occasional Sunday lunch free from the responsibility of their small children, who enjoy a sack lunch and recreation while their parents are socializing at a nearby restaurant. It also provides an opportunity for friendship circles to develop naturally between young adults and new members. Some other congregations offer this Sunday noon child care service every week, with paid nursery personnel and sack lunches provided by parents.

Singles. A group of single women in another congregation, most of them aged forty to sixty, have formed a "lunch brunch" after church on Sunday. The pastor says that this fellowship ministry counteracts the loneliness many singles feel most acutely when they eat alone on Sundays.

Visitors Pass the Word

American hoboes have a special code of markings they leave on back gates and barns to tell their friends good or bad news. Scratched with a knife or marked with crayon or chalk, these symbols can mean that food is available, that there may be danger ahead, or that you may sleep in the hayloft. This communication system dates back to the vagabonds of the European Middle Ages. It was brought to America by Irish tinkers and German immigrants. With the great migrations that occurred after the Civil War and again during the

Depression, these signs were an often-used language. Worship visitors do not leave marks on your sanctuary doors or parking lot curbs. But they do base their decisions on whether to return by how members act, and they tell dozens of people what they think of your church. Set your thermostat on friendly.

VI
Visit Your Visitors

Develop effective ways to encourage first-time worship visitors to return.

Earlier in this century, residents from the dry county on the north shore of the Ohio River often visited the wet county on the south side. One morning at about 2:00 A.M., an inebriated man climbed into his rowboat to make the return journey. He rowed strenuously. Time passed. Much time passed. Rays of sun tinting the darkness told him something was wrong. Looking over his shoulder, he saw that he had forgotten to untie his boat from the dock.

Success in many endeavors requires insight as well as effort. Growing churches work, not just harder, but smarter. No other single factor makes a greater difference in improving annual membership additions than an immediate visit to the homes of first-time worshipers. Failing to do that is like leaving a church tied to the dock. When laypersons make fifteen-minute visits to the homes of first-time worship visitors within thirty-six hours, 85 percent of them return the following week. Make this home visit within seventy-two hours, and 60 percent of them return. Make it seven days later, and 15 percent will return. The pastor making this call, rather than laypersons, cuts each result in half. An Episcopal church in Texas had forty-nine additions in a recent year, following several years in which additions had averaged thirteen. When asked what made the difference, the pastor said, "One thing. We got organized to make immediate home visits to first-time worship visitors."

In congregations in which laypersons do not call on visitors, 7 to 12 percent of first-time worship visitors eventually become members. In the average congregation, that rate runs 12 to 15 percent. With a good "immediate response" program, the rate of eventual joiners can rise to 30 percent. A few churches reach 40 percent.[1] Yes, ask the pastor to mail a note to all worship visitors on Sunday morning. Yes, a "get acquainted" phone call to the home helps. But neither substitutes for an immediate, personal visit.

This thirty-six-hour visiting principle derives much of its power from two contextual factors: (1) the new "church shopper" mentality among American churchgoers and (2) the feelings of loneliness and lack of connectedness among American people. An incredible 73.3 percent of new church members over the age of eighteen will say, "This is the best church" after attending several others.[2] One of the ways they form that opinion is by observing how much the members care and reach out to them. While we may radically disagree with this comparison approach to church choice, we cannot stop it. The church shopper syndrome shows no sign of going away.

Different visitors are looking for slightly different qualities in a church home. But every visitor seeks active acceptance. Everyone wants to attend a church in which people care about them personally. Expressing this with Sunday morning smiles and handshakes is important, but a home visit communicates active, rather than passive, caring. Worship visitors have said by their presence, "We like your church. We don't know how much yet, but we like it some." A home visit reciprocates with the unmistakable statement, "We like you, too."

A study conducted by the Lutheran Church in America found that among eighteen congregational characteristics selected as most important in choosing a congregation, fellowship and friendliness of members ranked in the topmost cluster.[3] A study in the Christian Church (Disciples of Christ) showed the same thing.[4] While churches can extend friendliness in various ways, nothing equals an immediate call in the home. Calling communicates caring. People respond to that.

A few active church members will protest with, "I would resent that kind of call." If you plan your program of evangelism by listening to their logic, you are managing by the exception to the rule instead of managing by the general rule. Six percent of persons called upon will not find these visits helpful. However, 28 percent of those called upon will find them somewhat helpful. Sixty-six percent of those called upon will find them very helpful.[5] Churches often allow a microminority of vocal, influential, dead-wrong leaders to move their congregation toward death by sinking the most effective outreach boat they can put in the water.

Organizing for Action

The best way to accomplish these immediate response visits is by recruiting a "Super Six Team;" if the church is larger, call it an "Awesome Eight Group" or a "Terrific Twelve Team." Ask each couple or individual to serve for a year. Give them some brief training in how to make these calls. Churches in large metropolitan areas can select people from various quadrants of town in order to minimize travel time. Ask these team members to meet for five minutes right after worship each Sunday morning with whoever takes care of the worship registration pads. That individual can glance over the forms and instantly spot first-time visitors. During those few minutes, team members decide among themselves the answer to the question of which one will visit the home of this first-time worship visitor, no later than Monday evening. Team members report back the following Sunday, using a card or "Master Prospect Record."[6]

Avoid asking the regular evangelism committee to become the "Super Six Team" for several reasons: Involving more people raises a church's evangelism consciousness, improves the extroversion climate, and increases motivation for assimilating new members. Additionally, this specialization of labor protects the program from faltering for several months while a new evangelism chairperson is getting organized.

Ninety-five percent of congregations using a "Super Six" approach prefer not to telephone for an appointment; they just drop by. The visit lasts only fifteen minutes. These people attended church that morning or the day before. That makes these visits warm, not cold. Many church leaders throw up their hands in horror at the thought of not phoning ahead. A quick check inevitably reveals that these leaders have had no experience in making these kinds of visits. Their fears are based on other types of visits, like those made by the pastor or calls on inactives. If an irreconcilable controversy arises regarding whether to phone ahead, propose an experiment. Make ten visits without phoning ahead. Make ten other visits after phoning for an appointment. This will prove what works in your particular community.

What should you say on these visits? Knock or ring the bell. Step back a pace. Say, "Hi, there. We are ———— from ———— Church. We are glad you visited our worship service. We can only stay a few minutes, but we wanted to drop by and get acquainted. I hope we haven't come at an inappropriate time." Ninety-nine percent will invite you in, unless it really is

75

an inconvenient time. If so, express your appreciation for their visiting worship. Urge them to come again next Sunday. Say you will catch them another time.

Once inside the home, remember why you came: (1) to get acquainted, (2) to answer any questions they have about your church, (3) to learn about their religious background and needs, (4) to leave them a brochure describing your church, and (5) to invite them back. Don't overstay. Fifteen minutes is plenty. If you stay more than thirty minutes, you should not have gone. People always have a planned use for their evening. Even if their plan is only to watch television, they will resent your stealing their time. Leave while they are asking you not to run, but avoid telling them you have other visits to make. That sounds institutional. It says, "You are not as important as other people." Rather, say, "We don't want to take up your whole evening."

If you visit on Sunday evening—which is the best night—you will find many people at home. If they are not home, leave a brochure describing your church in their door. This tells them you cared enough to come. Write a note on the back: "Dear ———, Sorry we missed you. We were glad to have you in church this morning. We hope you will come back next Sunday. (Signature)." Later in the week, follow up with a get acquainted telephone call. Since they know you attempted to visit them, this phone conversation produces some of the impact and much of the information you would have obtained in the home visit.

Print your church brochure small enough to fit into a regular business envelope, not more than a three-fold piece. Avoid making it large or several pages long. Do not approach homes carrying bulky material. This makes you look like a salesman. People seldom read thick information pieces at this stage, anyway. Save denser matter for later, after they have attended again and appear interested. On the front of your brochure, include a drawing or picture of the church building, the address, and the church phone number. Put a map on the back, showing where the church is located in the community. This allows the brochure to double as a promotional piece for people who have never attended. The inside section should list some of the church programs, particularly those for children, youth, and young adults. The human eye inevitably moves to the upper left of a printed page. That is the place to say, "Here are the spiritual and personal enrichment opportunities we offer you and your children." Avoid four paragraphs of denominational history. For most people, an interest in that comes later—much later. Make your initial communication "you focused," rather than "us focused." Other parts of the brochure can illustrate as much of two other qualities as you have space for: your church's caring ministries in the community and the biblical basis of its teachings.

Get the Names and Addresses

Immediate home visits are impossible without names and addresses. Several commonly used methods for getting these do not work. A guest register in the narthex seldom gets signed by everyone, except in the tiniest of congregations. Even there, the system malfunctions unless one person has dedicated his or her life to arriving early and pleasantly pressing everyone to sign. Visitor cards in the pew racks or worship bulletins seldom work well. Asking people to stand and introduce themselves raises negatives. Some visitors are shy or wish to worship anonymously (approximately 70 percent). Others are considering changing membership from another local church, so they do not want their presence circulated on the community gossip vine. Having worship visitors stand up (or remain seated while others stand) can subtly substitute an institutional system for genuine friendliness.

If properly used, a "Ritual of Friendship" pad consistently

obtains 100 percent of visitor names and addresses. Print that phrase at the appropriate point in your worship bulletin. The pastor should say something like: "One of the things we value most in our church is friendliness. We want to know one another and extend a friendly welcome to those who worship with us. In order to help us do that, the ushers will come forward and distribute a "Ritual of Friendship" pad. We ask that you all, members and visitors alike, write your names and addresses. (Avoid telling them to sign the registration pad. That word, *sign,* has negative psychological connotations from military service and school memories.) When the pad reaches the inside aisle, please pass it back to the other end, noting the names and addresses of persons who are seated on your pew. This will give you the opportunity to greet and get acquainted with one another after the service. The pastor must make this statement *every Sunday.* Expecting the method to work well without verbalizing it means you are not expecting any new worship visitors, who have never heard this motivational explanation.

"Ritual of Friendship" defines the name-and-address process as friendliness instead of as institutional manipulation. Since most people want to have a reputation for friendliness, that psychological desire counterbalances their resistance. Everyone is writing on the pad. Everyone knows that others will look at the names. This positive peer pressure even works with the approximately 20 percent of any crowd who enjoy resisting institutional systems. In a split second, they think, "Am I going to be the only unfriendly person on this pew? Not on your life. Let me sign that thing."

When introducing the "Ritual of Friendship" idea, outline its purpose to the church board, to key leaders, and to the adult Sunday school classes. Regular attenders cooperate with much greater enthusiasm when they understand that their "modeling" behavior contributes to the effectiveness of the church's evangelism.

Repetition Is Worth Repeating

In addition to immediate home visits, most growing churches make continuing contacts with worship visitors. Without those, many ships that would have docked will drift back out to sea. Do not expect these repetitive contacts to occur spontaneously. Everybody's business becomes nobody's business. Each of the following systems has worked in dozens of churches. Choose the one you feel best fits your congregation.

Persons Involved in Evangelism (PIE). Ed Kolbe, of Lincoln, Nebraska, developed and used this process to reverse a ten-year membership *down*cline into a ten-year *up*cline. Now widely copied into infinite variations, the basic program is: The pastor picks recruited volunteers from each regularly meeting adult group—the choir, adult classes, the women's organization, and so on. These persons serve on the PIE Team for one year.

Group members meet once each month and do four things at each meeting: (1) They briefly study some educational or inspirational aspect of evangelism. (2) They review the church's entire prospective member list. Team members accept assignments to make contact with those individuals before the meeting next month. They make these contacts in various ways. Some visit the home. Others phone. Some write letters. A businessperson may take another businessperson to lunch. A teacher may contact a teacher who works in the same elementary school. (3) They report to one another on the contacts they made during the past thirty days. Over a period of several months, three different team members contact each individual or family. (4) They eat *PIE*, which symbolizes evangelism in a positive way and facilitates the fellowship dynamic that gives team members their long-term staying power.

Several important by-products grow out of the PIE recipe.

Congregational friendliness increases as team members eagerly look for and greet the people in worship whom they have contacted. Extroversion increases in all adult groups, since each now has two resident consciences asking the question, "What are we doing in this group to reach out to new people?" Membership assimilation improves and back door traffic into inactivity slows. Often, new members become fully assimilated into a church group before they place their membership. Evangelism consciousness gradually rises as large numbers of members rotate through the PIE Team during successive years.

Weekly Calling Teams. In many large congregations, in which the number of weekly worship visitors is high, several calling groups, of ten to twelve persons each, work well. One rapidly growing congregation carefully selects and recruits eighty people each year. They work in eight teams of ten people each. Callers are chosen because of their outgoing personalities and their active involvement in the church. Each of the eight teams makes calls six to seven nights per year. The supervisor prints a calendar of the calling night dates at the beginning of each year. Some teams agree to call on Tuesday, others on Thursday, and so on. In order to ensure that calling occurs fifty-two weeks per year, regular calling nights are rescheduled during the months in which holidays fall on them.

If properly approached, 10 percent of active church members will participate in a visiting program. Without organization and training, nobody will. Do not issue a general invitation for all members to attend weekly or monthly calling nights. This never works. What would happen if you asked for volunteers to come each week and teach your Sunday school classes? The same principle applies to evangelistic calling. Enlist specific people to call on specific nights.

The following outline has worked well for developing weekly calling teams in many congregations.

1. Pick team captains, each of whom will lead a team of no more than twelve or less than six persons. Ask these captains to serve for one year.

2. Pick dependable, outgoing individuals with a proven track record of giving good attention to details.

3. In a congregation with an average of one hundred in morning worship attendance, recruit two teams. In a congregation with an average of two hundred in morning worship, you need three teams. With a congregation of three hundred in morning worship, use four teams. With six hundred in worship, organize eight teams. For the tiny congregation of less than fifty in worship, one team of four to six persons will suffice. But if you use only one team, it should meet for five minutes each Sunday morning to receive assignments and report back on calls, rather than coming to the church for a calling night during the week.

4. Call a meeting of the team captains and the ministerial staff. Review the membership list together, looking for couples and individuals you feel would make good callers. In extremely large churches, a meeting of teachers or key leaders of all adult Sunday school classes can help locate good callers.

5. After each team captain has acquired a list of twelve to eighteen potential callers, ask them to visit these possible team members in their homes to secure a commitment on a "Reach-Out Caller's Commitment Card." In these home visits, the team captains explain the rotational team system and stress the following ideas: "We know you may not feel like you know how to do this. Most people don't. But the pastor and the team captains feel you are the kind of person who can do an excellent job of representing our church. We have set up a one-hour training session to acquaint members of the calling teams with how to make these brief, friendly visits. If you attend this training

session and decide you do not wish to serve, we will understand. But we are certain that you will feel very comfortable in making this kind of call."

6. Schedule the one-hour training session several weeks after recruitment. This gives team members time to work it into their busy lives. Also, the further in advance you ask someone to do something, the more likely the person is to say yes. The six-weeks volunteer recruiting principle is that anybody you ask to do anything is likely to imagine that he or she will be much less busy in six weeks than right now. Make the training session a dinner meeting. Send out RSVP letters. Have team captains remind their team members with a phone call. Use name cards at each plate. Seat each team together. This allows them to get acquainted and to begin developing a team spirit. Present each person with an outline on paper of the ideas presented in the training session.

7. At the end of the training session, each captain should reconfirm the commitment of each individual or couple to serve on the team. Very few will decline. Work out the details of when the team will meet (every two weeks, once a month, and so on) to make the calls. The frequency and scheduling will, of course, depend on the size of the congregation. Some teams may choose Tuesday night for their calling; others may choose Wednesday, and so on. (any night except Friday or Saturday is fine).

8. Whatever calling team system is used, the pastoral staff, especially the senior minister, *must be present for all calling nights*. Without visible participation by their pastor, callers will begin questioning the value of the calling program. Most pastors find this easy to arrange, since they always have visits that need making. The practice of telescoping evangelistic calls into this one night each week enables the pastor to keep up with her or his end of the load.

Other Return Encouragers. Take instant-developing photographs of infants and present them to their parents in a cradle roll certificate. Take pictures of an entire children's Sunday school class each time a new visitor attends, then present it to the youngster on a printed card that says, "My Friends at ——— Church." Be sure you have one close-by parking space available for each two persons in average morning worship attendance. If severely short on parking, ask board members to park at a distance so visitors can find a spot. Multiple services that keep the sanctuary less than 80 percent full on an average Sunday encourage shy people who hate walking to the front. Mail a note from the pastor to first-time worship visitors on Monday morning. Insert a section in the worship bulletin every week entitled "Programs for Young Adults." A weekly listing of youth activities coming up in the next month encourages parents, whose church selection is much influenced by what the church offers for youth and children. Form a telephone committee of three to five persons who are highly skilled in talking on the phone. Organize them to make calls each Saturday morning to persons who visited the previous Sunday, giving special attention to those not found home in visits earlier in the week. Small congregations can recruit a group willing to invite second-time visitors to their homes or to a restaurant for lunch after worship.

Do not try to substitute these methods for repetitive personal contact in homes. The nonchurchgoer cannot be reached by the nongoing church. When pastor and people go to homes, people come to visit their church home.

The Ten Marble Method

A seminary president, desperate for help, asked a prominent insurance executive for his secret of success in building a large clientele.

"Ten marbles," the business leader replied.

"What do you mean?" asked the educator.

"When I graduated from college and went to work for an agency, I had trouble getting started. I was well educated—graduated magna cum laude and Phi Beta Kappa. I knew a lot about insurance, having completed the company's basic training school in Philadelphia with top honors. The town was growing. There was no shortage of young couples who needed the protection my company offered. But I wasn't getting anywhere. My monthly sales summary looked like the morning after a two-foot snowfall.

"After a couple of months, the man who owned the agency called me into his office. 'We are going to give you a raise in salary,' he said.

"'Really?' I replied, not able to hide my surprise. 'When does it become effective?'

"'As soon as you do,' he said, 'and that is why I wanted to talk with you this morning.'

"Reaching into his desk, he took out a small tobacco sack. 'Hold out your hands,' he said.

"I did, and he poured ten red marbles into my sweaty palms. He then handed me an embossed instruction card.

"'Slip this under the glass on your desk top,' he said. 'Read it every morning after you come to the office. The idea is simple, but like most truly great insights, it is easy to forget.'

"The card said: 'Put ten marbles in your right coat pocket. Go out and start calling on your prospective clients. Each time you complete a call, move one marble from your right coat pocket to your left coat pocket. After you get all ten marbles into your left pocket, you are finished for the day. Come back to the office, write up your reports, and go home—even if you haven't sold anything.'"

Do you want to lead a growing church? Attend workshops to increase your professional knowledge. Read books that sharpen your skills. But nothing equals ten marbles in effectiveness. Evangelism is much like football. Most teams do not lose because they have not learned enough fancy plays. They fail because they forget the basics. When churches are first established, members are aggressive extroverts. They intentionally reach out to people in the surrounding community. But after the church gets a few years older and about one hundred and twenty members tall, leaders begin to lose their marbles. Set up some kind of system to keep from losing yours.

VII
Friendliness Is Not Enough

Organize need-meeting activities for all age groups

A little boy came home from his first day at school. His mother asked how he liked it. "I hated it," he said. They put me in a room full of kids all by myself." Adults who join a church in which they do not participate soon feel that they have entered a lonely crowd. Sitting on the bleachers is fine at ball games. At church, it is deadly. Christians who do not participate either vegetate or evacuate. Churches that offer friendliness on Sunday morning, but nothing else, are making a five-foot jump over a six-foot hole.

In addition to facilitating personal Christian maturity, create *gossip evangelism*. When members are personally excited about the activities in which they are participating, the word gets around. If nothing interesting is happening, trying to attract new members with public relations techniques is an uphill climb. Synthetic good news pulls a poor response.

Methods of creating member involvement take different forms in different-sized churches. Small congregations are primarily people-centered. For members of small churches, being together as a family group provides personal involvement. Medium-sized congregations are primarily activity-centered. Involvement comes through participation in various church programs and activities. Large churches tend to be event-centered. Several months in the annual calendar have a "third annual this" or a "sixth annual that." Yet, all three sizes can offer ample opportunities for involvement and participation—providing leaders are intentional about meeting this need.

A Group and a Job

Members of a young congregation remember their first years as their best. They were meeting in a school, holding annual bazaars, and experiencing all kinds of frustrating inconveniences. But everyone calls these the "good times." Later, they lost this esprit de corps. Inactive percentages increased. Enthusiasm diminished. What happened? During the early days, everyone was involved in the group. Each person had a job to do. If they missed church, they were missed—and phoned next week.

Older congregations cannot manufacture climates that equal a new church birth; nothing matches that set of circumstances. When the unique challenges of those first years stretch into ten, they become a drag anyway. But growing church leaders know that opening the door to high member participation percentages takes two keys: a group and a job. Ninety percent of new members who do not experience these two things will be inactive at the end of the first year. New member dinners, pictures on the bulletin board, stories in the newsletter—these are all good, but nothing can substitute for being involved in a group and having a job to do.

Each time a 747 prepares for takeoff, the pilot and crew run a preflight checklist, not just any checklist, but the *right* checklist. Asking the wrong questions is extraordinarily unhealthy for everybody on board. Church officers can also improve long-range flight success by asking the right questions. The following list can significantly strengthen assimilation effectiveness.

Do we expect people to find a place by accident? Without some kind of system, "out of sight" can lead to "out of mind" can lead to "out the back door." Set up a welcome home assimilation system. Appoint one person, not a committee, the responsibility of helping new members find a place. Ask this assimilation officer to work with other key leaders to make certain all new members become quickly involved in a group and in a job. Ask your assimilation officer to report at each board meeting by maintaining and displaying a list of all new members on a poster board. Beside each name, note the job or role each person assumes, along with the class or adult group he or she joins. This keeps leaders constantly aware of and motivated to do their part in helping assimilate these new members.

Have we appointed a specific person the responsibility of discovering the talents and interests of all new members? The assimilation officer described above is the ideal person to do this. In small congregations, train a volunteer for this role. In large congregations, in which one hundred or more new members join each year, a quarter-time or half-time lay staff person works best. Use a "Talent and Interest Inventory," but do not leave it in the home. New members forget to return these, so avoid sending them in the mail. Avoid distributing them at a new member dinner. Make an appointment to visit the new member's home to deliver the "New Member Packet" (which contains various items to help get them aquainted with the congregation). Spend five minutes asking the questions on the "Talent and Interest Inventory" orally. People will be more likely to give information in this way than they would have done on paper.

Do we burn out older members and leave out newer ones?
Congregations usually have about sixty "jobs" available for
each one hundred morning worship attenders. The larger the
congregation, the greater the tendency to pile all these
leadership roles on a few key persons. This gradual centering
in is a normal result of three factors: (1) We tend to ask people
we know personally to help us. (2) We tend to ask people who
have proven their dependability in the past to help us. (3) We
tend to ask people we know agree with our viewpoints to help
us. This natural "running downhill to a smaller nucleus" tends
to burn out the hardest working core leadership group, while
reducing the involvement (and thereby the commitment) of
numerous other members.

Call together a group of long-term leaders. Distribute
membership lists. Write beside each name all the church
offices and roles each person holds. Jobs will cluster around
some people. Keep this list handy during nominating
committee meetings, other committee meetings, and cabinet
meetings during the coming year. You can involve many of
the persons who have white spaces beside their names.

Set aside an annual Sunday when the sermon deals with
spiritual gifts. Publicize it a month in advance. Rather than
asking people to help fill these jobs, the sermon should
concentrate on raising the question: "In what ways has God
gifted you for his service, and what is he calling you to do with
those gifts?" Ask worshipers to volunteer for the coming year
by checking a sheet that lists all the church roles and
committees. Do not set this Sunday in conjunction with the
annual financial campaign. Lumping the two together
weakens both results. Some people decide they can choose
between giving money and giving time. The New Testament
does not promote those options—it asks for both.

Never permit chairpersons to pick their committee members in isolation. Ask them to meet and review the
membership list, along with information such as that obtained

89

from a "Spiritual Gifts Commitment Sunday." Select potential committee members by working together as a team. This protects chairpersons from asking some members to serve on two committees while neglecting other people altogether.

Are we involving new members in a Sunday School Teacher Corps? This system simultaneously solves teacher recruitment frustrations and assimilates large numbers of new members. Different from team teaching, a group of persons takes responsibility for each children's class. New Teacher Corps members are recruited during the year, rather than only at the beginning of the year. Four, five, or more persons assist each lead teacher in three ways: (1) by serving as a substitute, (2) by assisting the lead teacher for one month during the school year, and (3) by teaching for one month during the summer.[1]

Do most of our new adult members join Sunday school classes? The "Magic Three Plan" draws up to 80 percent of new adult members into Sunday school classes. Ask each class to select a recruitment officer. During the first week after each new member joins, the pastor calls the recruitment officer in a class whose members have similar ages and interests as the new member. The recruitment officer makes a twenty-minute visit to the home of the new member to get acquainted, to say "We are glad you joined our church," and to invite the new member to his or her adult Sunday school class. The following week, another person or couple from the same class makes a similar visit. The third week, same play, different visitor. This organized extroversion helps new members feel wanted, while assuring the numerical health of adult classes.

Did 50 percent of current church officers and board members join our church in the past twelve years? While many persons who join a church are happy with a *follow*ship role, some want to lead. If they do not get that chance, they fade away and find a church in which they can.

Do we substitute committee work for participation in study and fellowship groups? Many small churches use an organizational structure designed for churches five times their size. This keeps members so busy running the organizational machinery that they have no time to participate in the opportunities for spiritual growth that the machinery is supposed to produce.

To combat this problem, many micro churches shift to a council system. They appoint the usual committee chairpersons, but instead of holding eight separate committee meetings each month, they call these chairpersons together for a monthly council meeting one week prior to each board meeting. Extremely small churches hold this council meeting only five times each year—September, November, January, March, and May.

At the council meetings, committee chairpersons take turns bringing up matters from their sections of church life. While each chairperson has the floor, the other chairpersons become members of the speaker's committee for those few minutes. This ensures democratic input and protects chairpersons from solo flights into ill-advised decisions. Following the council meetings, committee chairpersons ask other members of the congregation to execute specific tasks or events (such as planning the Christmas party). But each appointee's responsibility continues only for the duration of that project. Specific talent is thus used in specific ways, involving the whole membership in various activities throughout the year. Many people who refuse to serve on a committee for the entire year gladly agree to work on a specific project.

Do we provide ministry jobs as well as management jobs? About 15 percent of church members are leader types. They enjoy using logic and verbal skills. The other 85 percent get satisfaction from helping people, from helping with various tasks, and from helping the church succeed. They derive a neutral or negative charge from committee discussions.

91

These people are not kidding when they joke about not liking committee meetings. Most of them do not view making management decisions as a worthwhile use of time. Maximizing meaningful involvement in ministry and minimizing meaningless management time is thus seen as a plus by most members. Identify specific jobs and appoint specific persons to do them each year—for example, an electrician who takes responsibility for all property matters requiring that specialty, Sunday school teachers, greeters, one-to-one ministry to older adults.

Are we programming effectively for young adults? Approximately one-third of the population of the United States is between eighteen and thirty-seven years old. Church committees and boards, often composed of older adults, tend to overlook programs that meet the needs of this age group. The pastor of a growing church in Kansas says, "We targeted young adults as a group that we wanted to reach. We did this by starting new programs, such as athletics (which resulted in a number of couples coming into our church), improving our nursery, starting new Sunday school classes for young adults and children, starting younger youth groups and children's choirs, starting small group Bible studies, and so on. In short, we began to offer ministries that met their needs. Through the friendship factor, we were able to attract and keep many of them."

The easiest new group to develop is young married couples who have recently joined the church. The second easiest group to develop is older singles, many of whom are divorced. The third easiest group to develop is young career singles. The most difficult group to develop is college students.

Are we achieving our potential for reaching out to singles? In 1955, 2.4 million Americans were divorced. In 1985, twelve million Americans were divorced. At the close of 1984, 25.7 percent of all family groups in the United States consisted of single parents with children under the age of eighteen. One of the major differences between fast-growing and slow-growing mainline churches lies in their ability to attract these unmarried persons. More divorced and separated people join fast-growing churches. Almost twice as many never married persons join fast-growing churches.

More than seven million of the eighteen to thirty-seven age group in the United States are single. But mixing the six types of singles in the same group is an oil-and-water effort. Churches that try this mixing inevitably experience more frustration than success. The different groupings of singles are: young working adults just out of high school; young college adults; young, never-married, post-college-aged adults; young, previously married adults in the age range of 25–35; previously married adults in the age range of 35–55; and the sixth group of single adults is persons above the age of fifty-five who are either divorced, widowed, or never-marrieds. Churches with an effective singles program have usually capitalized on the predominant group in their congregation and have decided to focus on that particular ministry.

The larger the church, the easier it can develop a singles group. Singles are magnetically attracted to large groups. Hungry for relationships, they know they are more likely to find them in big churches. In establishing a singles ministry, give attention to obtaining a nucleus of leadership, rather than trying to find one person who is willing to teach a class. Help this leadership corps to recognize that singles work contains a built-in self-destruct mechanism. One-half of a successful singles group turns over every six months. The group grows by attracting new people. But if it succeeds in doing this, the participants often get married and leave the group. Singles groups that fail stay small and die. Groups that succeed are constantly dying, too. But they are constantly reborn by attracting new members.

Do we realize that new adult classes are the key to Sunday school growth? When mainline denominations were growing rapidly in the 1920s, adult Sunday school classes operated like evangelism committees. When evangelism committees replaced adult classes as the church's official outreach arm, Sunday school enrollments and church membership both began dipping. (To a large extent, the fast-growing Southern Baptist Church has avoided this denominational death trap.)

The most successful new classes are composed of young adults who have recently joined the church. Far better educated and more adept at verbal skills than previous generations, today's young adults prefer to discuss rather than to listen to lectures. Most classes, therefore, stop growing when they reach about thirty-five on the role and twenty in attendance. New classes also tend to close their doors socially at about eighteen months from birth. These are two of the many reasons new members are far more inclined to join new classes than existing ones. Large churches should launch a new adult Sunday school class every two years. Smaller churches need to establish a new young adult class every five to six years.

Do we organize multiple choirs? Most growing churches have two musical groups per one hundred average morning worship attendance. With one hundred worshipers, that usually means one adult choir and one youth or children's choir. With two hundred in morning worship, that usually means one adult choir, one handbell choir, one youth choir, and one children's choir. Even in congregations with five hundred in the morning worship, this ratio tends to stay about the same, if the church is growing. Choirs draw many children and youth from the fringes of church life who would not otherwise participate. Music programs provide the secondary benefit of attracting other family members into active participation. When choirs perform on Sunday morning, nonattending parents and grandparents usually appear. What if your small church lacks a music staff leader? Look for qualified people in the community who could direct your music ministry on a part-time basis.

Do we have quality youth work? All growing churches have strong youth programs. This inclines leaders and members toward confusing the causes of growth with the effects of growth. Good youth work is not so much a cause of church growth as it is a result of church growth. Most growing churches contain a large volume of families with children. The parents usually insist on good youth programs. Yet, if this need is not met, the church loses some of its magnetism.

Two factors have put greater pressure on youth work leaders in recent years. First, there have been smaller numbers of high school youth because of the birth rate decline. (Church members who are unaware of that statistic often see their smaller youth groups as a programmatic failure and blame the leaders.) Second, there is a greater insistence on quality from the baby-boomer parents. These young adults grew up with high expectations.

Here are some youth work tips: Keep youth and children's activities highly *visible* in bulletins, newsletters, and brochures. Church shoppers in large congregations (one thousand or more members) are especially likely to expect effective youth work and children's programming. Lower than average income church shoppers also have higher expectations regarding youth work.

Very few youth groups reach significant size and vitality unless they meet once each week. The occasional exceptions to this rule are metropolitan churches, which serve a geographically dispersed congregation whose youth attend many different high schools.

As a general rule, putting high school and junior high youth in the same group puts a lid on attendance. The total seldom moves beyond eight, with the largest percentage of attenders coming from the junior high age range. Mixing these two groups is practical only in small congregations whose potential attendance is limited to eight or fewer youth. In those situations, a family atmosphere holds the group

95

together. Older youth tend to treat younger ones as siblings, instead of seeing them as "those immature junior highs."

In regard to youth fund-raising, look for one or two big projects that require a great deal of group involvement and produce large income. These are far superior to car washes and bake sales, which require immense time and energy from sponsors and parents, but produce small amounts of money—for example, try an annual dinner theater, sponsored by high school youth; an "Eat Lunch with the Church Bunch," sponsored by junior or senior highs, held at noon on Sunday and featuring something simple to fix.

Do we have "quality" fellowship dinners? The larger the congregation, the greater the necessity of four to six fellowship dinners each year, with programs and/or speakers widely publicized. A quality program and the statement of a high purpose are essential. Dinners with a stated purpose of fellowship usually attract few church members; people are too busy these days to give themselves that luxury. But if some significant, worthy purpose is announced, they attend and enjoy the fellowship. Use variety. One dinner could raise money for the youth. Another might focus on a special speaker of significant national or local fame.

Have we tried capitalizing on Wednesday nights and working women? Some churches with poorly attended potluck suppers have discovered a better idea. A Texas church invented a "Dine In, Dine Out" program that has been widely copied in various forms. Each Wednesday during the school year, the church employs a local restaurant to cater a dinner, beginning at 6:00 P.M. and concluding at 6:45 P.M. People go through the line when they arrive, thus eliminating the frustration of waiting for stragglers. The fee for the meal is a small, break-even amount—cheaper than most families can eat at home. The church provides a nursery and attendants for younger children. Various study programs, committee meetings, and choir practices are scheduled during the remainder of the evening. Since members often invite friends to the meal, it has doubled as an evangelistic tool. It also gives the pastor an opportunity to visit informally with persons he or she could otherwise see only infrequently.

Have we responded to the new day in women's work? Church women's organizations that achieve large attendance rates usually structure themselves differently from those that succeeded in the 1950s. They concentrate on developing groups (circles) of individuals with similar interests, rather than identical groups that all study the same material. Women's organizations that attain a large size do, however, have a widely affirmed overarching goal and purpose. The support of foreign missions or denominational work, while still important to older women—is insufficient to attract large numbers of young women in this generation.

Are we benefiting from the current revival of interest in men's meetings? Men's groups need a valued reason for existing, such as making money at an annual barbecue for a widely affirmed cause. Most successful men's groups structure themselves around some sort of meal. Even then, few groups fly well unless two or three highly committed individuals make a large number of telephone calls each month to remind men of the meeting.

Are we reaching out to senior adults? The United States Census Bureau predicts that by the year 2000, the proportion of persons above age sixty-five will increase by 22.1 percent. In 1776, one out of every fifty Americans was over sixty-five. Today, one in nine has reached that age. By 2030, the figure will reach one in five. The four greatest needs of old age are: health (including safety and crime), financial security, a closer relationship with God, and a closer relationship with family. Other important needs are retirement and the use of leisure time.

Loneliness ranks high on the unspoken complaint list of many older Americans. Retirement halts work experiences, which provide a sense of positive self-worth. It also cuts people off from much of the human interaction that once brought meaning to life's hours. Many senior adults, therefore, suffer from a continuous low grade infection of loneliness, depression, and feelings of worthlessness. In Florida's trailer parks, doctors call the alcoholism with which seniors try to treat this pain "the silent death."

Possibilities for improvement through church ministries are: a senior travel group, which takes trips together on a regular basis; a monthly fellowship meal that provides women with the opportunity for social interaction and the chance to cook for someone again; some sort of "one-to-one" ministry in which church members commit themselves to maintaining continuous friendship contacts with elderly members, especially on birthdays and other special occasions.

Do we publicize our community service ministries? Most growing churches provide more service to their communities than do nongrowing churches. Often, they develop a reputation for a unique ministry that no other church in town has. This unselfishness simultaneously meets needs and attracts young adults. If your church is not reaching out in service to the community, do so. If it is already doing this, but is not publicizing it, do so. People cannot appreciate what they do not know.

Are we staffing for growth? Generally speaking, one full-time minister can care for a church of two hundred in average morning worship, although the ratio descends toward one hundred fifty as the average age of the congregation goes up. Having more older adults means that you have more single-person family units, more illnesses, more hospitalizations, more funerals, and more grief ministry situations. For each additional one hundred morning worshipers, add another full-time staff member, or the equivalent. Several factors cause the average congregation to require more staff per one hundred worshipers than in the 1950 decade. Among these are: changes to smaller family sizes, the loss of many volunteer church workers due to more women working outside the home, and a greater desire for professionalism in church life.

Several alternatives can meet this need in the awkward-sized church, which needs another staff person but cannot afford one. Employ a quarter-time person to do youth work (junior high through college age). Employ a quarter-time children's worker to cover all the programs for sixth grade and below. Employ a quarter-time person to care for the children's and youth choirs. Employing persons from within the congregation is always a little dangerous (relatives are easy to hire, but hard to fire), but leaders can minimize this danger by always employing part-time lay staff persons on a one-year contract basis, with the contract reviewed by both parties at the end of each year.

God's Network

An Atlanta based all-news TV station proclaims itself the "World's Most Important Network." That slogan really belongs to the church. People have four basic needs all their lives. Every person needs security. Every person needs to belong. Every person needs to believe that he or she has influence. Everybody needs self-esteem. When a church lives up to the potential God has given it, no organization does these things better.

VIII
The Message Is a Mighty Method

Concentrate on nurturing the spiritual side of human personality.

The full-page investment company's ad carried a color reproduction of Michelangelo's familiar painting. The bearded figure of God stretches his index finger across the vaulted ceiling of the Sistine Chapel in Rome to touch Adam's finger. Underneath the picture, the ad said, "Sometimes success is a matter of making the right connection."

During the 1960s, young adults started dropping out of the mainline churches in which they had grown up. Those who retained relationships with religious groups scattered in three directions: (1) to Eastern religions, which emphasized the mystical and spiritual; (2) to evangelical and fundamentalist churches, which emphasized Bible study and prayer; and (3) to Charismatic churches, which emphasized the Holy Spirit. All three groups offered a new alternative. They concentrated on nurturing the spiritual side of human personality. They went beyond the "rational optimism" which many mainline churches had promoted as the way of salvation since the 1940s. They went beyond the psychologically oriented human potential movement. They went beyond the "ecumenism is the answer" held up as a utopian dream by conciliar movement leaders. Mainline leaders often accused these groups of feeding on the weak personalities of people who had deep pscyhological needs. This oversimplified observation missed the target. These groups were setting spiritual tables in a time when people were intensely hungry for spiritual food.

Gallup Poll studies show major differences among members of various denominations, regarding how important religion is in their lives. Seventy-four percent of Southern Baptists and 71 percent of Mormons say that religion is "very important" in their lives. Only 53 percent of United Methodists, 46 percent of Presbyterians, and 42 percent of Episcopalians say religion is "very important" in their lives.[1] While no studies have compared how members of growing and nongrowing mainline churches would answer this question, the evidence indicates that growing churches have retained some of the spiritual focus their colleague congregations have lost. When invited to answer the question of "What does our pastor do best?" a layperson in a growing Eminence, Kentucky, congregation said, "Communicates a living God to people." Growing churches give people more than psychological help, more than good ideas, more than emotional experiences, more than a social group. They take seriously the spiritual side of human personality. They do not confuse the bread of life with the crumbs of religion.

Beyond Programs and Activities

Bob Gribbon of the Alban Institute says it is not just conservative churches that are growing. "We found that baby-boomers were most responsive to those congregations which had clarity about their central religious function—people don't come primarily for program, but for some connection with the transcendent."[2] This fits with historian

Martin Marty's observation that growing United Methodist congregations have recovered the "warmed heart" personal experience of Jesus from their Wesleyan heritage.[3] James B. Sauer echoes that when he says that three ingredients repeatedly appear in growing Canadian Presbyterian churches: (1) spirituality, (2) warm fellowship, and (3) evangelistic outreach.[4] Many mainline congregations' ambitious church growth programs fail because they leave out the first part of that holy trinity.

A Gallup Poll indicates that 87 percent of Americans pray some time each day. That figure includes 75 percent of those who are *not* members of a church or synagogue and half of the people who subscribe to no formal religion. In the past, people who prayed tended to be the aged, the sick, the poor, and those with limited educational backgrounds. Today, a growing number of well-educated, affluent, young adults find value in prayer.[5] That helps to explain why young adults respond positively to prayer trees, to prayer chains, to prayer circles, to prayer partners, and to daily prayer covenants. When American people ask what a church has to offer them, they think of the spiritual. Congregations whose major focus is something other than presenting spiritual reality in understandable ways do not fully meet their needs.

A little boy, during a cold Michigan winter, said, "Daddy, I wish you would make more registers all over the house so we would be warmer." His father knew they did not need more registers. They needed more fire in the furnace. Better organizational structure, "restructuring" denominational wall charts, adopting General Assembly resolutions—none of these replaces fire in the furnace.

Beyond Civic Religion

A laywoman reported that because of family moves around the country, she had transferred her membership to five different Presbyterian churches. "You are the first pastor who ever asked me about my spiritual life," she said to her new minister.

A layman in Ohio, when asked to list the major issues facing his congregation during the next five years, wrote, "Many people are committed to our church (its building, its need for a new organ, and other physical needs). There are many good, faithful Christians in our church. But as a whole, we seem to lack spiritual vitality."

A layman in South Dakota said: "This congregation has a serious lack of spiritual depth and commitment. Until this problem is rectified, any attempt at church growth (new members) is doomed to failure."

Churches easily fall into the routine of providing a social and psychological ministry to well-adjusted pagans, with whom questions about the spiritual side of life are never seriously raised. When that happens, lay leaders begin seeing their church responsibilities the same way they view their other community involvements; the church gets the same attention as the Kiwanis Club. Sociological pressures encourage this trend. Many small communities have about the same number of leadership roles as towns double or triple their size, but with a much smaller leadership pool on which to draw. Church leaders find themselves overwhelmed with community leadership responsibilities (many of which also meet fellowship needs). This can cause them to look at the church as one brick among many bricks, rather than as the cornerstone holding up all the bricks. When this pattern of "civic religion" is passed forward for several decades, only a determined modeling of new behavior by the core leadership group can move the church toward a spiritual focus. When that new "modeling" occurs, it is usually led by a pastor who emphasizes personal prayer development, Bible study, and the reality of God in personal life.

Beyond Rationalism

Numerous elements influence an individual's appropriation of the Christian faith. Tradition is one of these; the Roman Catholic Church leans heavily on this. The Bible is another; the fundamentalists draw much water from its well. Emotion is another; the charismatic movement is much in touch with and touched by its power. Rational thought is another key element in planting and shaping personal faith. A mainline leader describes the historic theological position of his denomination as a partnership between Faith and Reason. He says that frontier church leaders forged a synthesis of reason and revelation, a "rational supernaturalism."[6] That movement among all mainline denominations helped counter the sloppy emotional excesses of "revival religion," but it also planted a cancer in their bodies. When rational marries spiritual, it tends to gradually run spiritual out of the house. Together, the two produce offspring. Apart, they produce zero-based denominations.

This is another root cause of Sunday school decline in mainline churches. Without a spiritual focus, Christian education reduces to a discipline in which there is no objective truth, only subjective truth. That eliminates the possibility of a revealed truth from the Bible, which is supra-rational. *Bibliolatry* can block holy truth by putting it into inflexible, unusable, deadening form. *Rationalolatry* can block truth by being a sieve that examines all truth, but that holds onto none. Rationality declares that biblical truth is figurative truth. Spirituality declares that biblical truth is more than just figuratively true. As a Catholic missionary puts it: "The gospel is, after all, not a philosophy or set of doctrines or laws. That is what culture is. The gospel is essentially a history, at whose center is the God-man born in Bethlehem, risen near Golgotha."[7]

A political figure was described by the press as having an

overly emotional commitment to his rational ideas. That is currently the greatest danger among mainline religious leaders—an overly emotional commitment to their own rational thinking abilities. This masked form of atheism denies the presence and power of God by asserting that real truth is limited to the rational truth we can think up for ourselves. If God is real, surely he is bigger than our minds. If God is as real and power*full* as Jesus said he was, is it not irrational to think his truth is no bigger than our grasp of his truth? The spiritual is beyond the rational in a different level of consciousness, just as a parent's love for a child is in a different level of consciousness from his or her rational thinking about that child's needs. Parental love has rational components, but it transcends the rational as algebra transcends fourth grade arithmetic.

God's kingdom is a spiritual realm, not an emotional or a rational realm. It cannot be judged or appropriated by either the emotional or the rational side of personality. It partakes of both, but is not limited to either. Emil Brunner put it this way: "The better we know God, the more we know and feel that His mystery is unfathomable. The doctrine which lays the most stress upon the mystery of God will be nearest to the truth."[8]

Theologians and pastors who become overly emotional about Christian rationality commit the same error of which they accuse fundamentalists and evangelicals. When a lawyer asked Jesus to name the great commandment in the Old Testament Law, Jesus quoted the Shamah from Deuteronomy, chapter six. But he changed one of the words. He said, "You shall love the Lord your God with all your heart, and with all your soul, and with all your mind [rather than might]" (Matt. 22:37). When we try to live out Jesus' teachings, we must take care not to remove our minds from the endeavor. But we must take care not to make a god out of them either. C. S. Lewis said that "Christ plus" something else is the beginning of heresy. People inevitably become preoccupied with the plus rather than the Christ. Some parts of that insight are easy to see: Christ plus the Bible is bibliolatry. Christ plus patriotism is patriolatry. Christ plus denominationalism is denominationalolatry. Christ plus methods is methodolatry. Some other illustrations of that insight are not so easy to see: Christ plus a building is buildingolatry. Christ plus evangelism is evangelolatry. Christ plus ecumanism is ecumanolatry. Christ plus rationalism is rationalolatry.

Rational thinking, when divorced from the spiritual side of personality, becomes an almost invisible form of "salvation by intellectual good works." The Christian faith is neither right acting (as some conservatives would tell us) nor right thinking (as some liberals would tell us). It is right relationship, in which we allow our lives to be touched through a spiritual connection with God.

Beyond Emotionalism

The excesses of emotionalism have repeatedly damaged Christian believers. In late seventeenth- and early eighteenth-century Russia, for example, tens of thousands of "Old Believers" committed suicide, generally by burning themselves. Most of those were corporate deaths, taking place in hermitages or monasteries. In several instances, the number of persons who perished in a burned-out settlement far exceeded the number of deaths at Jonestown.

We must constantly hurl correctives against the perverted emotionalisms that cause these disasters. As Dietrich Bonhoeffer said, "God is not a God of the emotions but the God of truth."[9] But we must also avoid confusing a spiritual focus in church life with the extreme emotionalisms of fundamentalism, of Jonestown, or of the revival era. Because the spiritual side of personality is rooted in God rather than human feelings, it is as far beyond emotion as a Mercedes is beyond a bicycle in the field of transportation.

106

Beyond Ecumenical Universalism

When Charles Colson presented his testimony in India, the predominantly Hindu crowds nodded and smiled in approval. At first, this startled him. How could they be so amenable to what Christ had done in his life? He got a clearer picture when a Delhi pastor reminded him that Hindus believe all roads lead to God. If Jesus was his guru, fine. They all had their gurus, too.[10]

The ecumenical movement makes rich contributions to American church life, but its extremes have taken many "ecumeniacs" well outside its boundaries. Total tolerance and open-mindedness can become empty-headedness. Christians can end up thinking that what they believe does not matter. Although not its original intent, extreme ecumenism easily becomes a form of universalism that says there is no need to reach out for God or for any other form of salvation. Not all religious ideas are of equal value or equal truth. A bland ecumenism that says everything is okay is like putting out blank, signed checks on which every ideology and theology can draw. That soon depletes a congregation's credibility and effectiveness accounts. Ideas have consequences. Growing churches, though they may espouse ecumenism, move beyond it. Few people are attracted to a theological anything goes, in which a majority vote on God's truth makes it so. They remember that Jesus invited us to enter the *kingdom* of God, not the *democracy* of God.

Beyond Institutionalism

Sitting in a fellowship hall in a German Lutheran Church in West Chicago, a visitor observed several big wall banners idolizing the congregation's past history. One said, "Serving God for 100 years—1879–1979." That statement is simultaneously a cause of celebration and of fear. Churches that arrive at a certain age are tempted to look back with pride, pull up the blanket of secure institutionalism, and rock into the future, oblivious to the spiritual needs of the current generation. This pleasant deception, which works like slow doses of arsenic to congregational health, is surely one of the reasons why Presbyterian pastor Lloyd Ogilvie has said, "The central task of my ministry is to help religious people know God."[11]

Subsidence is a geological problem found in several parts of the country. Pennsylvania shopping malls often "settle" in places because of the coal mines that run under many of the towns. Houston, Texas, has the same problem for a different reason. Large volumes of underground water pumped out for use in the oil fields have created an estimated one hundred geological fault lines. The United Methodist Conference building in Houston is gradually sinking into the ground, causing cracks in the plaster and brickwork. In describing this slow-motion disaster, a staff person said, "The building has a solid foundation, but the whole thing is sinking."

Mainline denominations, built on solid theological underpinnings, are quietly sinking into historical oblivion. The major fault line is the shift in focus caused by pumping the spiritual out from under the foundations, leaving only the organizational, social, and political plaster to hold up the buildings. Why do so many conservative churches have no systematic annual financial campaign, yet seem to have plenty of money? Because their message is a mighty method. They do not need a system because they have never substituted organizationalism, institutionalism, or civicism for a continuous call to spiritual commitment.

Beyond Christian Unity

An evangelism leader in the conciliar movement says that Christian unity is Jesus' strategy for world mission. "I am not quite clear yet how Christian unity can actually evangelize," he says. "But that is what I would like to work on."[12]

He is not alone in that lack of clarity. Christian unity is an admirable goal. History is sweeping all American denominations in that direction. But history tells us that concentrating on unity alone results in declining denominational membership. C. S. Lewis was right. Christ plus something else leads to heresy. It also leads to ecclesiastical extinction, even when that "something else" is as virtuous as Christian unity. In the mainline congregations that grow, most of the pastors believe in both these good ideas—Christian unity and evangelistic outreach. In declining congregations, the pastors often get locked up in the first of these and locked out of the second.

Beyond Social Action

A pastor asked a seminary student what she was majoring in. "Ministry to oppressed people," she said. Paul did a lot of that, too, but he would hardly have defined his major in such a specialized way. Jesus said the main thing in religion is to love God, and the next most important thing is to love people (Matt. 22:36-39). That order is no accident. Reversing these two produces a ministry of social actionism that looks meritorious but diminishes the chances of long lasting results. The fruits of the faith do not have the same power as the roots of the faith. Both are essential, but neither can substitute for the other.

Ideas have consequences. Why should we be surprised at evangelism's present low ebb in mainline churches? When you tell pastors and laypersons for thirty years that the second commandment is the main idea, they start believing and acting on that. This emphasis has given Christian humanism its tremendous appeal. By putting the second commandment first, Christian humanism appears to care deeply about

109

people. Ultimately, however, this great reversal brings us to not caring about people, as practical atheism begins replacing the first commandment. Environmental impact statements have become important to industrial planning. Denominations should require theological impact statements to help predict how a shift in teaching may affect the vitality of future church generations.

The New Testament church did its work in four different ways: *kerygma* (preaching of the Christ event), *didache* (teaching of new believers), *koinonia* (nurturing new Christians through fellowship), and *diakonia* (caring service). Healthy churches in all generations act like a clock whose hands keep sweeping a face containing these numbers. If the clock stops on any one of these, it loses its power to minister. The John Calvins and John Wesleys of history focused on all four types. When church leaders, as they did in the 1960s, begin limiting their work to one or two of these ministries, they are committing a heresy. It is, however, a self-limiting heresy. Leaders who expound such a truncated gospel eventually disappear. Their theology does not reproduce.

Beyond Church Growthism

The church growth movement is making major balancing contributions to mainline Christianity. It reminds us that real Christian faith is extroverted, not introverted. But church growth fanatics must continuously remind themselves that Christianity is not a method but a message, a message about the spiritual side of life. The Christian faith does not derive its enormous people-changing power from sociological principles. Its primary potency comes from theological truths, such as being born again (John 3:3), finding God (Acts 17:27-28), knowing God (I John 4:7-8), knowing Jesus Christ (John 1:1-14), knowing the Holy Spirit (II Cor. 1:22), and prayer (James 5:16).

Beyond Conservatism

Our caricatures of why conservative churches are growing fall short of total truth. Conservative churches do not grow merely because they are conservative. If that were true, the buggy whip manufacturing business would be growing. Nor are conservative churches growing because they send people on guilt trips. Nor is it because their simplistic messages and dogmatic doctrines free people from the need to think. Nor are all conservative churches and denominations growing; some are shrinking. The conservative congregations that are growing do so because they give the gospel message to people in ways that help them relate to God. Yet, some liberal congregations are doing the same thing.

How We Got off the Track

Keeping a church focused on its primary task is a complex leadership role. Several pressures push us off the track: (1) Each new crop of pastors is a "Ford Generation"—they inevitably think they have a better idea. In trying to assert their identity, they disdain the focus of the just-past generation. The 1950 to 1980 generation of pastors thought their ideas were better than those of the 1930 to 1960 generation of pastors. Now, a new 1980 to 2010 generation of young pastors is rediscovering a biblical/spiritual focus. This third group, in reacting against the thought patterns of the second group, is reaffirming the efforts of the first in new ways. (2) National and regional church leaders build their reputations by coming up with new ideas, not by promoting old ones. Thus they tend to discard automatically what worked for church leaders in the last generation. (3) Bishops, synod executives, and regional ministers focus their attention on the maintenance of institutional systems rather than the energizing of personal relationships with God. Immersed in institutional work rather than people's needs, they spend their days trying to balance budgets and to make clergy appointments. It is easy to lose your way in a paper wilderness.

Every institution exists to provide a service, a product, or an end result. When that institution becomes ineffective in its primary mission, it begins to die. If it does not recover its ability to provide that service, product, or end result, it does die. Pastors and denominational leaders must continually ask themselves, "What is our *primary* business?" If the answer lies in the direction of helping the largest possible number of people relate to God in a life-changing way, the denominations and congregations will grow. If pastors get confused and concentrate on "Christ plus something else," their denominations and congregations shrink and eventually die. God does not let weeds grow in the garden of his kingdom, but he does not chop them out. He lets them wither.

Søren Kierkegaard told a parable about a man who was walking down a street in Europe many decades ago. He saw a sign in the window that said "Pants Pressed." He went into the store, slipped behind the counter, and started to take off his trousers. A clerk saw him and said, "What are you doing?"

The man replied, "I want to have my pants pressed. I saw your sign in the window."

To which the clerk replied, "Oh, we don't press pants here. We just paint signs."

The signs churches erect on their lawns proclaim great heritages of Christian faith. The people who live in these buildings must keep asking themselves, "Do we help people find God, or do we just paint signs?"

IX
No Substitute for a Pilot

Have a pastor who facilitates and models magnetic
congregational qualities.

For twenty years, Ralph Tasker, of Hobbs, New Mexico, has repeatedly produced championship high school basketball teams. No matter what kind of player talent filters up from elementary school, he makes them into winners. Ralph Tasker Arena is a brick and steel monument to a principle that extends far beyond sports. More than any other single element, the coach makes the team. Church growth stems from many different factors, but none is more important than the pastor. A high quality flight crew cannot substitute for a pilot who knows how to fly the plane.

Vision

We can now list with assurance several pastoral qualities essential to leading a growing church. None of these is more important than vision. "After decades of developing rational theories of leadership, scholars are recognizing that great organizations are made by legendary leaders who focus a vision of human values which inspires, shapes and grows people."[1] Successful leaders have vision and communicate it, continuously, repetitively.

Commitment to the Primary Task

Pastors of growing churches come in many different shades of theological perspective—conservative, liberal, middle-of-the-road. But they all share one common trait, their unwavering commitment to the church's primary task: to help the largest possible number of people decide to follow Jesus Christ with all their hearts, minds, souls, and strength. Their internal drive to work at this task arises from different sources. Some are motivated primarily by the generalized desire to help people find a richer, fuller life. Others are motivated by a motif of pastoral care that believes Christian faith is the best way to heal hurts. Still others list the Great Commission mandate as their primary motivation. Yet, the observations that pastors of growing churches make about the church's main mission all come down to the same thing.

"If evangelism is not our primary concern, then we are in the wrong business."

"Evangelism is the business on which all other church businesses depend."

"It was the last thing Jesus asked us to do, and it has become the last thing our churches do. This must change."

"Jesus did not say, 'Love me.' Nor did he say, 'Serve me' or 'Respect me.' He said, 'Follow me.' And then he went out. He expects us to do the same."

Because pastors receive so much pressure to lead in several other directions, only the strongest maintain an unwavering focus on that objective. Part of this pressure comes from trying to lead the four kinds of members found in every mainline congregation. About 25 percent of members feel negative about evangelism efforts. These people do not want their church to do that sort of thing. They are not just unmotivated; they are demotivated. Another 25 percent of church members are apathetic. They feel evangelism is fine for other people in the church, but not for them. They are positive at the attitude level, but passive at the action level. Another 49.5 percent think the church should work at evangelism, but they do not personally know how to do this. A large proportion of this positive group operates with a handicap in theological perception. They believe evangelism is something the pastor should take care of, not laypeople. The final .5 percent of church members have the "gift of evangelism." They are actively and effectively influencing people in their community toward Christ and the church. Leading this membership mix is like trying to direct a band that continually marches off in all directions.

Another often mentioned pressure is the question of when pastors can find time for evangelism. Wrong question! Finding time is never the real problem. Time does not get lost. Right there on the clock in plain view, it is readily available for all to use as they choose. People sometimes lose sight of their primary task, but they do not lose time; everyone has the same amount. Busy professional people often say, "I am overcommitted." More frequently, the opposite is true. They are actually undercommitted. They feel overcommitted because they are undercommitted to the most essential aspects of their work. Busy people are prone to confuse the important parts of their work with the essential parts. All the essential parts are important, but not all the important parts are essential. The important tasks *should* be done. The essential tasks *must* be done. Pastors who recognize that evangelism is one of the essentials find time to do it.

115

A man drove into a service station and said, "Fill it up with unleaded, please."

"Can't do that," the young man said. "We have plenty of gas, but we don't have any power to run the pumps." Christ is the power source for evangelism, not the pastor. But the pastor is the power cord. If he or she is not plugged in, nothing happens—and the customers eventually stop stopping by.

Willing to Lead

Pastors have immense power. Even by his or her silence in a board meeting, authority is exercised. Most of the time, lay leaders try to do what the pastor wants done. They show equal enthusiasm for neglecting matters in which the pastor does not show interest. Nowhere is this more true than in evangelism. Almost everyone is comfortable with putting it on a forgotten far back burner. We must have morning worship and a sermon. We must have some kind of Sunday school. But if the pastor exerts no leadership in evangelism, few board members will hoist protest flags.

In describing a painter, someone said his talent had petered out in a passion for painting pebbles to give his friends to use as paperweights. When that happens to a pastor's determination to lead in evangelism, a church has little hope for the future. "If the pastor doesn't lead, the flock won't follow!" one pastor said. "Effective evangelism requires money, tools, and people," another said. "But will is more important than any of these. If the pastor does not have the will, the people never will."

Martin Marty says, "I can't overestimate the need for ordained clergy that are extremely sensitive to where people are but are not content to leave them there."[2] Stephen K. Wilke, describing the attitudes and management traits of fifty pastors of growing United Methodist congregations, said they showed "tremendous clarity" about why God had established

116

the congregation they serve and the pastor's role in fulfilling that purpose. "These pastors are mostly proactive rather than reactive," he said. "They present a very different profile from the ministers I usually work with."[3] A clinical psychologist's remarks, regarding the growing church pastors he tested in the Christian Church (Disciples of Christ), parallel that description. He said they use an "iron hand in a velvet glove" style of leadership.[4] The same principle applies in growing black congregations, but in a different way. In order for black churches to grow, they need pastors who combine aggressive community activism with a "Baptist-style" approach to the faith.[5]

Pastors of growing churches do not confuse administration with leadership. Every pastor engages in both tasks, but these are never identical. Administration is what happens in a church *after* leadership has been exerted. Unless that leadership continues in a strong way, administrative work grinds slowly down to small inconsequential matters, repeated endlessly. Leadership creates ideas, movements, momentum. Administration keeps tidy what leadership has launched. Administration says, ". . . all things should be done decently and in order" (I Cor. 14:40). Leadership says, "Where there is no vision, the people perish" (Prov. 29:18 KJV). Without it, churches perish, too.

Pastors of growing churches provide evangelism leadership in two specific ways. The first is theological. Evangelistic motivation and methods are fueled with theological conviction. Members who feel God is calling them to reach out to new people are far more likely to put their shoulders to the task. Over the long haul, this theological nonmethod is one of every growing church's most powerful methods. If the pastor does not provide this theological leadership, who will?

Second, pastors of growing churches provide leadership by helping church leaders develop an effective plan. Roger Staubach says, in his book *Time to Win*, that preparation is a prime element in football. He feels that that is one of the Dallas Cowboys' greatest strengths. They are very prepared. Churches do not win without a plan. Ordinarily, that plan is not the first one they try. They and their quarterback-coach have worked it out over a period of years.

Pastors of growing churches are eclectic in their willingness to try and/or discard evangelism ideas. They read books. They attend workshops. A layperson in Colorado describes pastors of growing churches as "truth seekers." He says these pastors, unlike those who are sure they know it all or those who are sure there is little to know, are always asking questions. They continually seek better plays for their church and community context.

Style and Behavior

People do not get a chance to pick their biological parents, but they can choose the parent figures to whom they relate. The following list may not include all the qualities of a magnetically attractive pastor, but they are among the most important.

Positive attitude. Nothing so immediately influences congregational direction, mood, and atmosphere as pastors who model a positive outlook on people, on reality, and on the future.

Enthusiastic. A church cannot excite new people without a pastor who is excited about its potentialities. This is especially true of young adults. They look for excitement in all parts of their lives.

Sense of humor. Cartoons collect more followers than turpentine bottles. Church shoppers assume that "as the pastor goes, so goes the church." More people want to join a happy group than a somber one.

Hope-full. People who dispense this quality are God's answer to valium—and almost as addictive. When people find this

118

quality in one pastor but not in another, guess whose church they join?

A caring, understanding listener. Some pastors overlearned and overapplied this trait during the 1960s. Enamored by the new pastoral psychology movement, many concluded that good listening skills were all they needed. But this idea can be undercooked as well as overcooked. Parishioners soon stop listening to leaders who stop listening to them. Pastors who exhibit warmth, care, sensitivity, affirmation, and empathy soon have more and more people with whom to practice these skills.

Spiritually focused and biblically centered. People who attend church are looking for a relationship with God. If they were looking only for a pleasant experience with other people, they would attend a football game. If they were looking only for a chance to help a good cause, they would give to the Cancer Fund. "She gets us thinking about the spiritual side of things," an Ohio woman said in describing her church's director of Christian education. People already have ample opportunities to think about the rational and emotional sides of life. When a pastor sets up signposts pointing toward the spiritual, people respond.

In communication, the medium through which the message is transmitted is often the strongest part of the message. In evangelism, the message is a person—Jesus Christ—who is primarily transmitted through the medium of other persons, especially pastors. A relationship with God is not so much taught as caught through experiential contact with a *Christed* personality. Truth can be conceptual (God is love). Truth can be metaphorical (God is like a good father). Truth can be personal (let me tell you about my relationship with God). Pastors of growing churches communicate all three types of truth, but they are especially gifted at the third.

Entrepreneurial. Some pastors of growing churches have a mildly introverted personality. Others are extroverted. But all

119

are entrepreneurs. The good news is, after all, a proclamation, not just a listening ear. Pastors who do not strongly believe they have an immensely important message to communicate—a product to give away that everyone in town needs one of—seldom influence many people toward Jesus Christ.

Positive appearance. A middle-judicatory staff person who had worked with pulpit committees for ten years said that all their concerns boil down to five questions: (1) Is he easy to talk with? (2) Can he preach? (3) Does he make calls? (4) Does he get things done? (5) Do his socks match? "Cleanliness is next to Godliness," someone once said. So is neatness. If the package is unkempt, people may not move close enough to examine the contents.

A winsome style. The St. Louis airport houses one of the world's finest shoe shine shops. The young men who work there have entertainment ability unequaled by most stand-up comics. From the time a customer enters, a continual stream of anecdotes, quips, and jokes flows above the shiny wax and snapping cloths. Customers are drawn there for the experience, not just for the shine. The upbeat atmosphere convinces them that the shine will be fantastic. On the other hand, if the shine were not superb, the entertainment would not keep people streaming back. Pastors need both style and skill. What a pastor does is important. What a pastor is ranks as equally important. Pastors of growing churches exhibit both style and ability.

A high energy level. Evangelism does not happen by ease or by accident. You cannot microwave it into a church in three minutes. A denominational executive says, "Only pastors with high energy levels are successful in starting new congregations." The same is true of pastors who recharge the batteries of older congregations. You cannot get results without work. If nothing goes out, nothing comes in.

Perry Gresham, president of Bethany College in Bethany, West Virginia, was fond of saying that when someone told him

120

they had happened through Bethany College on the way to somewhere else, he knew they were stretching the truth. Nobody ever happened through Bethany College; it is too far off the beaten track. Nor does anybody ever honestly say, "Our church just happened to grow." Evangelism does not happen by accident while you are on the way to someplace else. You have to intend to get there. And if the pastor doesn't intend to get there, no one else in the church will get there.

Denominational Officials Can Lead, Too

"It is difficult for even the most intelligent people to hold two good ideas in their minds at the same time," a psychiatrist wisely observed. We have seen that principle operating in American Christianity during the past thirty years. A few denominational leaders have encouraged their churches to concentrate on local service (ministries of pastoral care, evangelism, and fellowship). But most denominational leaders have led the church in concentrating on distant service (ministries to ghettos, of political action, and to the starving in countries like Ethiopia). Which is the right choice? Both! Balance! God calls the church to work both out there and in here. If it does not concentrate on distant service, a church compromises its integrity. If it does not concentrate on local service, a church commits slow-motion suicide and thereby compromises its ability to deliver distant service.

Local pastors listen to the oral and the paper smoke signals sent from denominational leaders. These executives exert far more influence on the actions and priorities of local churches than they realize. If they do not row the boat in a balanced way, it eventually turns over.

Transmissions Unlimited

A pastor sitting in a coffee shop one morning in Richmond, Indiana, noticed a husky man sitting three booths away. The bold letters across the back of his blue shirt said, "Transmissions Unlimited." The pastor's eyes shifted back to his coffee cup, then looked again. *Hey,* he thought. *Transmissions Unlimited. That's the business I am in.*

Transmissions have no power of their own. Their job is to transmit the power they get from somewhere else. Countless people in every American community live out their lives at a dead stop. When touched with the life-changing power of Jesus Christ, they can move ahead. Is that not our primary task? If we don't do it, who will?

Notes

I. Throw Your Message to Wider Receivers

1. Cynthia W. Sayre and Herb Miller, *The Christian Church (Disciples of Christ) New Member Study*, a study initiated by Harold Johnson, executive for the department of evangelism and membership of the Division of Homeland Ministries of the Christian Church (Disciples of Christ), Indianapolis, November 1985.

2. Warren J. Hartman, *Discipleship Trends*, December 1983 (Nashville: The General Board of Discipleship, The United Methodist Church).

3. Lyle Schaller, quoting Gallup Poll statistics in "The Erosion of Denominational Loyalty," *The Parish Paper*, 1985.

4. *Emerging Trends*, vol. 7, no. 10 (Princeton, N. J.: Princeton Religion Research Center), December 1985.

5. "Lutheran Listening Post II" (Philadelphia: Office of the Bishop, Department of Planning, Research, and Evaluation, Lutheran Church in America, August 1982).

6. Ronald Schiller, "How Religious Are We?" *Reader's Digest*, vol. 128, no. 769 (Pleasantville, N. Y., May 1986), pp. 102-4.

7. Statistics generated by the General Assembly of The Presbyterian Church (USA).

8. *U.S. News & World Report*, "Church Rolls State by State," Oct. 11, 1982, p. 13.

9. *Emerging Trends*, vol 5, no. 1 (Princeton, N. J.: Princeton Religion Research Center, January, 1983).

II. Is Your Church Inviting?

1. John S. Savage, *The Apathetic and Bored Church Member* (Pittsford, N. Y.: LEAD Consultants, 1976.

2. Herb Miller, *Coming Home for Christmas*. This six-week process reactivates approximately 15 percent of inactive members. The same program has been successfully used by many churches under the name of "Coming Home for Easter." When it is used during the Easter season, the final dinner must be held on Palm Sunday, not Easter Sunday. The two-hour training module found in this program is also valuable for training leaders in "preventative" inactive work all year long. The booklet and cassette tape, which guide leaders in conducting the program, may be obtained from the NEA Resource Center, 5001 Avenue N, Lubbock, TX 79412. (The program should not be confused with a very different kind of program of the same name used by the Roman Catholic Church.)

3. Bob Burt, *Growing Plans* (N. Y.: United Church of Christ Board of Homeland Ministries, Division of Evangelism and Church Extension, June 1985).

4. *U. S. News & World Report*, October 11, 1982, p. 13.

5. Raymond J. Bakke, "The Battle for the Cities," *World Evangelization*, vol. 12, no. 42 (Charlotte, N. C.: The Lausanne Committee for World Evangelization, March 1986), pp. 10-16.

6. *Net Results* (Lubbock, Tex.: NEA Resource Center, October, 1985).

7. Ibid.

8. Charles Allen, address at the National Evangelism Workshop, Amarillo, Tex., May, 1980.

9. Martin Marty, *Context*, 1984.

10. Cynthia W. Sayre and Herb Miller, *The Christian Church (Disciples of Christ) New Member Study*.

11. Ibid.

12. The Gallup Organization.

13. Lyle Schaller, "You and Your Unchurched Neighbor," *The Lutheran Standard*, January 4, 1985.

14. Cynthia W. Sayre and Herb Miller, *The Christian Church (Disciples of Christ) New Member Study*.

15. Ibid.

16. For a free demonstration tape and brochure, write: *Radio Bright Spots*, 5001 Avenue N, Lubbock, TX 79412.

17. Curtis L. Keith, Jr., *Church Television Commercials: You Can Do It Too*, (Lubbock, Tex.: Net Press, 1985).

18. For a set of thirteen ads, send twenty-five dollars to: LifeStream Evangelism, 7275 South Broadway, Littleton, CO 80122.

19. Two of these are: Reaching the Newcomer (P. O. Box 640, Grapevine, TX 76051) and Dataman Group (1140 Hammond Drive, Suite B-2140, Atlanta, GA 30328).

20. Research done in August 1985 by National Family Opinion Research, Inc., for the American Lutheran Church.

III. God's Power Plant

1. Cynthia W. Sayre and Herb Miller, *The Christian Church (Disciples of Christ) New Member Study*.

2. Gallup International, *Faith Development and Your Ministry* (Princeton, N. J.: Princeton Religion Research Center, 1986).

3. Carl F. Reuss, *Survey of Lutherans* (Minneapolis: The American Lutheran Church, 1985).

4. *Webster's Ninth New Collegiate Dictionary* (Springfield, Mass.: Merriam-Webster, 1983).

5. Sheron C. Patterson, "Four Impediments Cited by Pastors as Barriers to UMC Ethnic Growth," *The United Methodist Reporter*, Dallas, Tex., February 28, 1986.

6. Don Shelton, "Little Things Make a Difference," *Net Results*, May 1986.

7. Richard Stoll Armstrong, *The Pastor-Evangelist in Worship* (Philadelphia: The Westminster Press, 1986), p. 16.

IV. Forward to Basics

1. *Emerging Trends*, vol. 7, no. 10 (Princeton, N. J.: Princeton Religion Research Center), February 1986.

2. Ibid, December 1985.

3. T. S. Eliot, *Four Quarters* "Little Gidding" in *The Complete Poems and Plays* (N. Y.: Harcourt Brace Jovanovich, 1952), p. 145.

4. *The United Methodist Reporter*, "Lutheran Scholar 'Sprinkles' Methodist Advice," March 28, 1986.

5. Roy Oswald with Jackie McMakin, *How to Prevent Lay Leader Burnout*, (Washington, D.C.: The Alban Institute, 1984).

V. Set Your Thermostat on Friendly

1. Warren J. Hartman, *Discipleship Trends*.

2. Ibid.

3. David Jones, *Reader's Digest*, January, 1985.

VI. Visit Your Visitors

1. Institute for American Church Growth, Pasadena, California.

2. Cynthia W. Sayre and Herb Miller, *The Christian Church (Disciples of Christ) New Member Study*.

3. "Lutheran Listening Post Summary" (Philadelphia: Lutheran Church in America, March 1977).

4. Cynthia W. Sayre and Herb Miller, *The Christian Church (Disciples of Christ) New Member Study*.

5. Institute for American Church Growth.

6. Available from denominational publishing houses or from the NEA Resource Center, 5001 Avenue N, Lubbock, TX 79412.

VII.   Friendliness Is Not Enough

1. For a complete description of this plan, see "One Solution for Two Problems: The Teacher Corps Concept," *Net Results* January 1984.

VIII.   The Message Is a Mighty Method

1. *Emerging Trends*, vol. 8, no. 1 (Princeton, N. J.: Princeton Religion Research Center, January 1986).

2. Bob Gribbon, "New Hints about Ministry with the Baby Boom Generation," *Action Information*, vol. XII, no. 2 (Washington, D.C.: The Alban Institute), p. 18.

3. Martin Marty, "Lutheran Scholar 'Sprinkles' Methodist Advice," *United Methodist Reporter*, Dallas, Tex., March 28, 1986.

4. James B. Sauer, in a publication of the Committee on Church Growth to Double in the Eighties, Presbyterian Church in Canada. Exact source unknown.

5. Ronald Schiller, "How Religious Are We?" *Reader's Digest*, May 1986, p. 102.

6. D. Duane Cummins, ed., *Disciples Theological Digest*, vol. 1, no. 1 (St. Louis: Christian Church (Disciples of Christ), Division of Higher Education, 1986).

7. Vincent J. Donovan, *Christianity Rediscovered* (Maryknoll, N. Y.: Orbis Books, 1982), p. 31.

8. Emil Brunner, *The Christian Doctrine of God*, vol. 1, trans. by Olive Wyon (Philadelphia: The Westminster Press, 1980), p. 117.

9. Dietrich Bonhoeffer, *Life Together* (N. Y.k: Harper and Row, 1976), p. 27.

10. Chuck Colson, "A Message For All Seasons," *Jubilee* (Washington, D.C.: Prison Fellowship, March 1986).

11. Lloyd Ogilvie, address at the National Evangelism Workshop, Amarillo, Tex., May 1980.

12. Raymond Fung, "A Monthly Letter on Evangelism," no. 4/5, April/May 1986, World Council of Churches, Commission on World Mission and Evangelism.

IX.   No Substitute for a Pilot

1. David L. McKenna, *Renewing Our Ministry* (Waco, Tex.: Word Books, 1986), p. 21.

2. Martin Marty, *United Methodist Reporter*, Dallas, Tex., March 28, 1986.

3. Stephen K. Wilke, "Clerics Giving Guidance Show Uncommon Traits," *United Methodist Reporter*, Dallas, Tex., May 23, 1986.

4. Bill Erwin, *Net Results*, November 1983.

5. Stephen K. Wilke, "Clerics Giving Guidance Show Uncommon Traits."